Searching for OZ - The Journey Home

By

Michael Cavallaro

& Adele Saccarelli Cavallaro

Illustrations by Jennifer Albright

Cover Design by Hafsa & Mohamed LOTFY

Searching for OZ - The Journey Home

An Adjunct to the Novel, *Searching for OZ*

"As someone who has read a number of self help & spirituality books it was a welcome change to read a flowing tale of a woman finding herself again in the form of a modern day fairytale. Adele's writing cleverly interweaves Dottie's own story with the characters of the Wizard of Oz. The story embodies the same magic of the original. Dottie quiets her thinking mind, moves forward with courage & reconnects with her heart to integrate childhood trauma. With the help of friends & a mentor Dottie is able to remember who she really is, which allows her to bring her gifts into the world. The book finds the balance between darkness & light. The reader watches Dottie learn new tools & knowledge that help her to reassemble her past so that her present & future are filled with light. I found the story particularly relatable in that having a guide and help were essential parts of my own story of remembering." *Jacqueline Renan*

"Sometimes in an author we recognize a voice, startlingly familiar, as if angels have guided their pen to page... tap, tap. I find myself engrossed in Adele's book, feeling honored that she would "share" her inner thoughts with me. I want to take her words in slowly and ponder them all, for I was meant to read this. Adele's style of writing is one in which the flow of words, although seemingly random, form beautiful, rhythmic patterns, like the movement of water in a stream. This smacks familiar to me. It is a voice through channels unexpected, that reminds me of home." *Judy Gubinski*

Dedication

To the World: We have created this guide (and coursework) with the intent of bringing a deeper awareness of trauma/abuse in all its forms to light with the hope of making real change.

Where there is Abuse, there is no chance for love.

For those who want to experience pure self-love...this is for you!

Acknowledgements

A special thanks to Michelle My Belle and Kaitie Lady:
> To Michelle for assisting us in the production of this book and connecting us with all the right people! - Freelance Designer, michstarke@gmail.com
> To Kaitie for encouraging me to continue on my life's mission to give others HOPE that there is life after trauma and to bring about changes that will end abuse in all of it's forms.

To all of our beautiful children: Lissy, Cassie, Timmy, Joey, Michelle, Kaitie and all of our grandchildren.

To all of our friends that have continuously helped with this work: Barb, Gail, Lynn, Phyllis, Pat, Deb, AnnMarie, Nancy, Shinjini and Abby.

To Mo, Leslie, Linda, Cassie and Kathy for your ongoing support and advice.

To Megan for amazing editing skills, and so much more. sublimedesignsmedia.com

To Liz for her patience & amazing formatting skills - bettyannedesign.com

To Jennifer Albright for her beautiful ideas and illustrations!

Liability Release

The *Searching for OZ* guide material and coursework is not therapy, nor is it intended to be. Although it may have therapeutic impacts because we do deep process, it is not intended to replace help from professionals of any kind.

By reading and/or agreeing to read this guide/coursework, you agree and understand that the *Searching for OZ* guide and in-person/online coursework is not intended as a substitute for the medical advice of physicians or mental health professional. The reader should regularly consult a physician and/or mental health professional in matters relating to his/her health and particularly with respect to any symptoms that may require diagnosis or medical attention.

You also understand that this could be triggering for those who are in the process of healing, a recovery, or still in the throes of the impacts of any trauma.

If you feel like you are in a place where you are well enough to take a look at the challenges in your life and personal story without it sending you somewhere you don't want to be, then we welcome you. If after reading this liability release, you have decided that this guide/coursework is not going to be right for you, you may request a full refund.

By reading further/ beyond this page I agree that I have read and understand fully this Liability Release. I agree to release *Adele & Michael LLC* and any parties connected with the *Searching for OZ* guide/in-person/online coursework from any lawsuits.

Thank you!

Michael Cavallaro and Adele Saccarelli-Cavallaro

Table of Contents

Welcome!

We have written this guide as an adjunct to the novel *Searching for Oz,* for those who want to go deeper in their healing and/or with the purpose of assisting others in their healing process.

In this guide, you will find answers to the healing of any type of abuse or trauma. The answers and processes you will read about are experiential and have been used by hundreds of people effectively and are the sole property and license of Adele and Michael LLC. The information and stories you are about to read are unique and work with traditional therapy, while also achieving a deeper and more permanent healing than traditional therapy that typically treat only the symptoms and is limited to coping with of the trauma of abuse.

Much of the groundwork for this process can be laid out and achieved during traditional therapy. We are not saying that this process is better than traditional therapy, only that it is an adjunct that takes you beyond the limits of traditional therapies.

Whether you choose to use this process or not, we wish you well on your journey to recovery and that your recovery places you in a far better and more conscious state than you were in before your trauma. You deserve it!

In this guide, we will suggest many things outside of the box. We would like you to understand that we are never implying that anything you experienced is invalid, only that there may be other perspectives to assist you in your healing. At times, we will suggest ideas and concepts that go beyond what you may have known. These things may at times seem harsh or difficult to swallow and yet at the same time, they will produce the opportunity for you to raise your consciousness and heal your soul.

The things that we suggest in this guide are intended to provide an opportunity to change from the inside out; to have peace within and feel true freedom from your Core. We will be using the word, "transformation" to replace the word, "healing" as we feel this is a more appropriate word. Healing implies that there is something broken and needs to be fixed. You are not broken. Transformation means to change in condition, nature, or character. We feel this is a more fitting word for any journey of change.

With much love and respect,

Michael and Adele

This guide is an adjunct to the novel *Searching for OZ*.

I originally wrote *Searching for OZ* to complete me; to impart the knowledge and wisdom through the writing for me. At the same time, it is to give HOPE that there is LIFE after a trauma.

Searching for Oz is a creative and informative book. It is a fictional account of the Wonderful Wizard of Oz theme that conveys healing information for anyone with a history of trauma or abuse. It is based on a true story, my story. Throughout the book, I shared the events of my truth from my perspective of how I mentally and emotionally perceived my life and my traumas. I had accepted these perceptions as my truth up until now.

As long as I had the wounds of abuse, there would be no chance of freedom within. When there is abuse, there is simply no chance for love.

This guide is designed as a step-by-step guide to finding your inner voice and transforming abuse and discovering self-love. It is written in a heartfelt and inspiring way, intended for anyone who has experienced trauma or abuse, of any kind.

I wouldn't have the peace inside today and the love that I deserve if Michael, my husband and co-developer, hadn't shared this beautiful life's work with me. From the time that I met Michael, he has modeled self-love, focus and precision of this process for change. He has shared with me a way that I could truly love myself again. If he hadn't, my story might not have ended so beautifully. I applaud him for this beautiful work.

I hope that by understanding, feeling and sharing your own story of abuse through the exercises in this guide, you may experience your own peace and love within!!!

Adele

This guide is based on the Transformational work that I have developed over the last 40 years. The self-discovery and transformational wisdom throughout the guide is actual real life information used with hundreds of people that I worked with who were on the journey to self-discovery and transformation. While working with people who have been abused and/or traumatized, Adele and I came up with six common stages that most people experience during the transformation process.

The 6 Stages in the Abuse Recovery System

(1) The Memory
(2) The Choice
(3) The Experience - Feel to Heal
(4) The Experiential Roadmap
(5) The Beliefs and Identity - "The Four Building Blocks"
(6) Clearing Your Beliefs - The Transformation

In order to free yourself from the wounds of trauma or abuse, you must allow memories of the trauma or abuse to surface, no matter how distorted they are. We have heard hundreds of stories of trauma/abuse and how we humans hurt each other, not to mention what you have personally experienced. No story is too unbearable to admit or look at, even if it seems so. It always revolves around your own judgment as to how painful the memories are. Keep in mind that the experience of the trauma or abuse in all actuality is the most painful and that memories only relive the experience through the mind giving the illusion of continued pain and suffering. This is not to say that the memories are not painful! I have helped many men and women find their way "home," back to peace, back to contentment inside, back to OZ! There has been no trauma that has not been able to be resolved with this work. The point here is that there is hope and all you need is commitment and application to your own self-discovery. I know that if you apply, there will be a chance for freedom from pain for you! You have to give it your all, if you want freedom from the trauma. You have to be fully committed. Do whatever it takes. Adele was one of those people that was willing to do whatever it took to have peace internally, to feel the love and contentment within, a peace that everyone deserves. I watched her determination over the years, plugging away at each part of her experiences to find her transformation to internal peace. You can too!

Together, Adele and I created this process that we feel would incur the least amount of pain and is the fastest way to freedom within, peace of mind and an open heart. Personally, I have always been about expediting the process of transformation, yet making sure it is permanent and as painless as possible. I hope you find this process beneficial to your human experience and soul, most of all I wish you a wondrous loving journey and a beautiful life experience.

Michael

Adele: Expediting the process of healing is something that Michael and I have discussed for years! One of the things that he always used to say was, "Wait, let's figure this out now, so we don't have to repeat it, love." It was usually during one of our quarrels, business decisions or something as stupid as who didn't close the coffee container.

Michael: That is true! But let's make something very clear, Dear, you were usually the one that caused us to have stale coffee. ☺

Adele: When you give it your all and you commit to finding your freedom you may perceive things as painful at times. But along with the pain comes a new sense of self and a release from the heaviness of the trauma and eventually the experience of joy that was long forgotten. You deserve for that joy to return! Ha!

Throughout this guide, you will hear each of our voices.

- Together, we will explain words like, judgment, rumination, controlled experience, your identity, keeping secrets from yourself, ownership, unwitting participant, ego, being free from limitations and returning to self-love.
- We will educate you about core programs, family patterning, and belief systems.
- We will walk you through the memory process, your choice of moving forward and the "how to's" of feeling to heal.
- We will help you to identify the beliefs that are specific to your situation; show you how to trail back to your specific family patterning and finding answers that will change your life forever.
- And then most importantly, <u>direct you to how you can clear those beliefs, which will bring you peace; the peace that you so absolutely deserve.</u>

<u>Ready to begin your journey home and find your own answers?</u>

What we mean by this is speaking and acting from the heart, your soul, your gut and your intuition. From the deeper recesses of you that feels fulfilling and complete, your "real" truth and knowing.

Meet Dorothy and the gang:

Brian
(Brain)

Tim
(Mann)

Leo
(Courage)

Dottie
(Short for
Dorothy)

They may be of some assistance to you throughout this guide!

Chapter One

It's Always Best to Start at the Beginning

<u>You may have questions about why your life is the way it is!</u>

Why me?   Why do I have this trauma?   Why wasn't I protected or loved?

Why did I deserve to have this happen?   What is wrong with me that this happened?

These are all legitimate questions that we have heard over the years.

<u>YOU have the right to ask ALL of these questions!</u>

<u>First you need to know that you did not deserve the abuse nor was it your fault!</u>

How did I get here?

It is important to ask yourself this question because in this process, which is about to be explained, you will need to know about your past.

To know your past, you will need to understand how you were shaped as a human being, and why your personality and identity are the way they are. Knowing how you were treated externally and how you perceived it internally <u>is required</u> to be free from the trauma inside.

This is not about judging those who shaped you. Throughout this process, it sometimes may be difficult in say anything negative about the people who raised you, especially about the parent that you perceived as the<u> less</u> abusive.

So it's *<u>not about judging anyone</u>*, rather this is more to understand and dismantle all the judgments and beliefs <u>that you have complexly and often unwittingly accepted as your truth.</u>

<u>Why are you **now** searching for something different?</u>

This question is about how you feel internally (both the feelings admitted and those unconscious or denied) and all of the effects from the abuse and the results of the trauma that have manifested in your current life's challenges and difficulties.

Just remember, you had experiences and <u>created beliefs</u> based on those experiences doing the best you could at the time when you were a small child.

The fact that you are here, at this moment, reading this, indicates that you have decided to delve into your own journey of transformation and self-awareness.

At this moment in time, somewhere inside, you have decided that the way you feel inside is not satisfactory and that there must be a better way to live life.

We congratulate you on being in this place!

However, in this place, you must realize it is only the beginning.

- Some people are here simply doing research and have not yet decided if they want to move further into their own transformation.
- Others are here ready to take "the bull by the horns" and actively apply all that they will learn and discover.

Either way, being here now is part of your journey. It doesn't matter if you're simply deciding or you're actively applying this, it's simply a great place to be.

You have identified the fact that somewhere inside
of you the way you feel is not satisfactory.

Below is your **first step** to The Seven Steps to Freedom!

Seven Steps to Freedom (1)

Knowing that you are unhappy where you are and having the desire to change

We want to define the word "unhappy" only because most people will say that they are pretty happy in life.

Unhappy - the state or feeling of unfulfilled or unsatisfied

Unhappy, for our purposes, means that your life is not fluid – almost effortless and enjoyable or fulfilling every day.

Most people define unhappy as "my life has to be complete misery and/or life is falling apart."
Most people settle for guilt, shame, fear, sadness, disappointment, unfulfilled or just to exist.
We do not believe that anyone should have to live this way!

<u>This guide is for everyone, not just for people who are really struggling.</u>

We are shining light on the fact that "normal" is not and should not be "struggling to exist by being satisfied by what you have."

<u>This guide is for those who would like to go beyond this feeling.</u>

<u>Never be satisfied by that which is unfulfilling or limits you!</u>

Think of this guide as the springboard to your new life!

If you are willing to see these hidden parts of "unhappy", this book is really for you!

Having guilt, shame, fear, sadness or disappointment is very common, the question is...do you still want to live with these emotions?

Face your fears and your doubts.
Press forward by continuing to read, and you will succeed.

Defining trauma and abuse:

Trauma - the internal label of a deeply disturbing experience.
Abuse - the external label of cruel and violent treatment of a person

We want you to know that we use trauma and abuse synonymously because from our experience one is the internal experience and the other is the external perception. Trauma/abuse can be mental, emotional, sensate, physical, sexual or spiritual. In this definition, there is no human being who has not experienced trauma/abuse and there is no way to have an abuse without a trauma. However there can be a trauma without a visible abuse.

No one must live with trauma/abuse!

It is your birthright to live with love and joy!

You deserve to have a life you love!

Having a fulfilled, satisfying life is <u>your birthright</u>!

**No human being can have true peace within
without understanding themselves!**

Here's a life changing question:

Who am I?

Simply put, you are a beautiful divine essence covered by a collective of core programs, patterned behaviors and belief systems from which you have determined your current identity.

Wow does that sound crazy or what? Actually it is a truth never given enough attention.

You have judged yourself based upon core programs and beliefs systems that you unconsciously decided were truths and most of which are not even your own. You have judged yourself to be a good person, a bad person, a successful person, a fearful person etc. There are an infinite amount of judgments and creative ways that you find to judge yourself in order to support the belief systems you think are yours. But you may not even be aware that these exist. Nor you may not realize these judgments are only made up by you; the judge and jury of your life.

The truth is in most cases, what you believe and what you judge about yourself is not even yours. It is simply something you were taught, you heard, assumed to be true and made part of your identity.

This may sound a little outlandish to some of you but, if you read on, you will begin to see yourself differently and understand yourself more deeply.

Some of the things you will read may sound familiar or inviting. Some of the things you will read will stretch you to the edges of your belief systems and beyond. Please do your best to read this book with an open mind and absorb anything that may serve you even if it sounds weird at first.

<u>You are something far greater than you are aware of right now.</u>

Come with us now on this journey as we share with you, new or not so new, understandings and wisdom – a process that has worked for hundreds of people successfully.

If you find it beneficial: live individual coaching is available, simply contact us for more information.

Michael: Adele will begin by telling you her story, something that we will ask you to do later on in this guide. You will need to spend the time to feel your past and the perceptions that you have created about your life experiences. This may sound unimportant but you will begin to see that your past holds the keys to your future.

Adele's story:

As a small child, I would check out of my body to disassociate from my feelings, because I didn't like how my outside world felt. I found it very difficult to stay present while with my family because it was quite intense. I tried living in their intense lifestyle and rhythm, but my focusing, transitioning and communication abilities couldn't keep up with their pace.

We were all taught to "give of yourself and sacrifice for and to others in the family" which was very common in the culture of the day. The problem with this was that my needs, desires and wishes were always second at best. This created a belief system that everyone came first before me and I believed that I had to fight or surrender what I wanted in life.

Ultimately it taught me to emotionally surrender myself to the wants, needs and desires of others before I could even consider getting my needs met. This went along with the catholic beliefs of "sacrifice myself and help others first," which they used to support this way of living. Really all this meant was that I wasn't the most important and I had no voice until everyone else had their say.

My first memory was around the age of **three or four**, I remember clearly "floating out of my body" at this age. I found it safer to leave my body, not being present, than to endure the intensity of my family. Only people that know how to leave their body will understand this completely.

So, at a very young age, I appeared unfocused. I spent the beginning of my life watching the family members around me, rather than living with them. I would hear a lot of "get focused or pay attention, Adele." I was labeled as being spacey and not focused.

A lot of times, I couldn't keep up with the conversations. I would hone in on everyone's behaviors and gestures and then guess at what they were saying. I would nod my head a lot, pretending to know what they were talking about. I did my best to pretend that I was living and participating in my birth family's world, of which I never really felt like I belonged. I stayed focused as much as possible within this intensity, then I secretly would slip out and float out in space.. So basically, I was in and out of my body.

My second memory was around 1970, when I was about **five** years old. It was at this time that I learned to hide; first from the family intensity and then eventually from the feelings of sexual abuse and grooming.

I got up from my bed and followed the sounds of music that I never had heard before. It was coming from my older sister's bedroom. It drew me towards the stairway. I walked down the stairs, stopping halfway down and sat on the step. I followed the music; the music felt soft, like a lullaby. It permeated my soul.

These songs were played one after another. From Carole King, *Beautiful*, the 5ᵗʰ Dimension, *Aquarius/Let the Sunshine In*, and *Let It Be,* by the Beatles and Joni Mitchell. All the music sounded and felt like love. This music guided me directly to the space that I used to escape when it got too intense, that I spoke of earlier. It stimulated and awakened something inside of me.

I naturally merged into the music. It allowed me to float and feel safe.

When things got chaotic or too intense in my home, I would go to that step where I sat and would feel the energy of the music, even if the music was not playing. The physical feeling of my buttocks, thighs, calves and feet on that particular step and the visual of the front door where I gazed when I first heard the music was enough to recreate the experience.

Then in 1972 at the age of **seven** years old, I was taken to my first Broadway play, *Jesus Christ Superstar.* Again, I recognized the energy of music. It moved me. The sounds and the lyrics of the love of Jesus and his mother were captivating. This rock opera was about the last seven days in the life of Jesus of Nazareth. I felt the love that was conveyed by the actors.

In 1978, at the age of **thirteen,** my mother took me to see *Ain't MisBehavin*, a sassy and sultry musical about the 20's and 30's. The sounds of the beautiful African women belting out soulful blues/jazz which permeated every cell in my body.

After that, when I would hear similar types of music in the car, at a friend's house or at a concert, I would recreate that same feeling. Music and floating in and out of my body was a way to escape and cope with the intensity of the family, sexual abuse and grooming.

In school, I was labeled ADHD, a dyslexic with auditory processing difficulties. All of these labels made sense because I floated in and out of my body so naturally I would miss auditory and visual information. *Again, only people who know how to float out of their body would understand this phenomenon. It works exceptionally well during labor/giving birth.*

As I got older, I realized consciously that I gave myself away to music, as well as to the people around me and it worked for me. Anything that became intense in my life, I would find a way to give myself away to it; anything not to feel the energy of intensity. If something got intense, I would divert the conversation. If someone felt anxious, depressed, disappointed or anything that made me feel uncomfortable I would try to mend it. I would do anything to change it for them, even if it meant giving myself away.

My feelings of sexual abuse and grooming:

One of my family members sexually abused me when I was **six** years old. Here is where love, touch, intimacy and sex became all mixed up. I loved this family member. This experience affected almost every aspect of my life. Touch had a distorted meaning. Love meant giving myself away. True trust, closeness and intimacy were non-existent. This was where I believe that my perceptions of things became distorted, from feelings of touch to the letters "d's" looking like "b's" to "k's sounding like "g's." This is also where I learned to move and talk fast to avoid feeling the memory of what was done.

The sexual act was quite direct. This family member was straight forward. He just held my head down for me to perform a sexual act until he was done. It happened three times.

The day before I was **thirteen** years old, my father died. A priest from school volunteered to come help out, by counseling me. I was having some difficulty with my dad's death because I had not known that he was sick and I was so surprised when I heard the news. He had been quite impatient with me because of my AD/HD and communication behaviors, so we didn't really get along, to say the least. We had our special moments, but there were not many of those. I tried to please him, chased him for his approval of me and wanted him to like me. Well, in my eyes, that never happened and at thirteen, after hearing the news of his death, there would never be a chance again. So when this nice priest offered his help, I accepted.

The very first time that I met this nice priest, I felt that invisible feeling of love (like the music that I felt and mentioned earlier! It felt safe), although it was mixed in with an underlying motive.

The priest displayed a spiritual type love, alongside sexual undertones. He would gazed into my eyes longer than was appropriate. Every time I would see him, he would project into me, as if he could see inside of me. It was like he went through my eyes and landed there and didn't leave. He was a touchy and feely with me, just preparing me for later, when he seemingly planned to come for me at a later date. Again, I wanted him to like me.

This is what we call grooming, folks.
(Grooming will be discussed in detail at a later time in guide)

Turns out he worked the circuit of all the surrounding grade schools, staying in touch with pre-teen and teen girls all the way through until my high school years. He became the chaplain for our high school. Then strategically, he would invite the high school girls to the rectory and the camp retreat buildings to mix that spiritual love with sex. I still have one of the letters of invite. I was fortunately, one of the lucky ones that didn't put myself in a situation for him to take advantage of, although there were at least four of my fellow high schoolers that I know of who were not so lucky. He is now in a "treatment" center for pedophiles run by the Catholic Church. Which I discovered was actually a sanctuary where they protect the pedophiles from prosecution.

When I was **fourteen**, the same kind of grooming happened similar to the priest, but this time, I wasn't so lucky. One of my coach's helpers, who was also her brother and a counselor at another school, helped out at our practices. He displayed the same kind of love, but closer to the love concept that I felt on the steps – peace –love –music. He displayed the behaviors – make love, not war, the kind of love attitude from the late sixties/early seventies music. He often bowed with his hands in a prayer-like way and spoke of love. I bought into it. I wanted him to like me as a fourteen year old.

I recognized this feeling very clearly. Every time I would see him, he would project into me, as if he could see inside of me. It was like he went through my eyes and landed there and didn't leave. After confiding with the head coach, she recommended that I talk to her brother, the counselor.

After one of the team counseling sessions, I asked him for some help. I drove to this counselor's house many times to be counseled by him, without my mother's consent. This man counseled me on sexual abuse. Imagine that, a groomer counseling on sexual abuse.

He felt very different during the counseling sessions. He didn't behave the same as he did during our team practices and out-of-school activities with the coach, such as rock climbing.

First, he had an emotional charge about the abuser, calling this family member that abused me, 'evil.'

The love and peace attitude he usually displayed was nowhere to be found.

Second, he made a comment during one of the counseling sessions that made me feel very uncomfortable. He told me a story of how he got an erection when his young niece was sitting on his lap. I froze, held my breath and pretended that he didn't say it. I wanted him to like me. Disregarding inappropriate grooming behaviors is normal for someone who has been sexually abused as a child.

I didn't realize until much later that I was only seeing this counselor ACTING like he understood this pure love. Not being aware that he was using it for his own personal gain. He may have wanted to be this love (I will never know), but I was told several months later from a neighbor that I should stay away from him because he got in some kind of trouble for messing around with some girls at the school where he worked.

From the age of **fourteen** until **twenty,** I had compared him to every guy that I met. No one measured up to the perceived peaceful love that he continually displayed to me.

Then at twenty-years old, I decided to profess my love to this counselor. I took a trip down to his house, during one of my college breaks. We sat outside on the grass on his blanket as I talked to him about my first real relationship. I was just about to explain to him that I had been in love with him since I was **fourteen** years old. Before I had the chance to tell him how I felt, he suggested that we go to his bedroom. I followed him in.

He then started kissing me. As soon as he kissed me, it felt weird. It felt like I was kissing the family member who sexually abused me. I ignored this uncomfortable feeling and also pulled away to talk to him about the love. I was just ready to profess my love, and he says, "Don't get too serious on me," like he knew what I was going to say.

My heart dropped.

And then he makes a comment about his fiancé joining us for a threesome. I was devastated. I was so embarrassed. I left. I went back up to my college and I wanted to hide. I wanted to get numb and forget everything that had happened.

He called me a couple weeks later and told me he was on his motorcycle, close to my college.

I felt embarrassed. I felt wrong. I felt that I had disappointed him when I left him at his house, a few weeks back. I let him down. I felt obligated to please him. You see I was taught like many others that my worth and value come from pleasing others, making sure they are happy and satisfied so they will then care for or love me.

As a young child, I learned to please, keeping everyone happy in order to keep them off me. I did it well. Although, if I wasn't able to please someone, I felt their disappointment, which then in turn, disappointed me because I wasn't doing my job--my job in this existence is to please.

Since I felt this obligation to please, if people approached me with an undesirable request, I often allowed them to take advantage of me in some way in order to gain their approval.

I allowed this counselor to take advantage of me. I let him in to my apartment at college that day. It was like being sexually abused at six years old all over again. I shut down. After that day, I withdrew and placed another layer over my heart.

A couple months later, I met my future husband. He was safe. He had gone through the same thing that I did as a child, it was a perfect fit.

I invited my coach and the coach's brother to my wedding. And I also asked the priest who is now in the treatment center, to perform the ceremony. I beat myself up for a long time because I invited them both. I asked myself, 'Why the hell did I do that?' I never even gave it a second thought, that is how unaware I was at the time. My symptoms and behaviors of sexual abuse will be explained later in this guide.

As a small child, I believed that love meant giving myself away. This misperception of love worked to my family member abuser, priest and counselor's advantage. This set me up to be taken advantage of.

After this particular experience , I became numb and shut down and suppressed all those feelings from the past.

<u>My new perception of love was cemented into place after this experience. Love meant that I must give myself away to receive it. What I thought was love was not. Everything turned out to be disappointing. For me, this changed what I believed about love.</u>

It wasn't until I was about thirty-three years old that I had finally reached the point where my life was no longer satisfactory, nor could I continue pretending that it was.

One day, an internal tornado of feelings ripped through me, so much so, that it felt as if I lost all sense of reality and logic. Well, not literally, but I did decide to wake up and change my life.

It had been about a year and a half since I made the move back to Pennsylvania from Kansas with my husband and two children.

I began taking a prescribed stimulant medication, for my inability to focus. I was finally ready to deal with my spinning ADHD mind, inability to focus, difficulties with communication and the fear of transitioning. This pill woke my ass up, well, woke my mind up! Ha!

All my life, I had never been able to sit still long enough or slow down my mind enough to feel things. Although, this medication kept me hyper-focus. which was great for my mind but not so good for my feelings and intuition.

Being on these meds allowed my mind to not only focus better, but also to question everything in my life. My mind wanted to place all aspects of my life in order, including my childhood traumas.

I had dealt with certain parts of these traumas, but this time, my mind wanted to reveal all of what was there. With each day that passed while on the meds, my new organized, medicated mind had a desire to organize, understand and resolve those feelings of trauma..

My new ability to focus filled my every waking hour with anal retentive tasks. Everything in my external life began to be more orderly – work, bills and my kids' schedules. The meds created focus and productivity, so much so that I went from being last in my company as a sales recruiter to first. I started to question everything in my life and then began to dismantle everything that was not working.

The more I delved into the feelings that I was having, the more my husband and I distanced ourselves from each other. Unfortunately, the marriage did not work out and we separated and then eventually divorced. Although I was able to make the transition of separation and the logistics quite unruffled, the feelings of ending a ten-year marriage were tough to handle.

I was decisive and determined and had made a choice to end this way of surviving. This new improved mind allowed me to look at the memories in order at which they occurred. I had tried therapy in the past, but it only took me so far. No one had the real answers to this wounded feeling inside of me that kept gnawing at me.

I asked questions to myself such as, "How did I get here? Why am I here? Who am I?"

Was there even a solution out there? Where would I begin the search?

In an effort of self-discovery, I began by revisiting my past only to find that I had no way of retrieving any clear answers and solutions.

In fact, I realize now that one of the main reasons I moved so fast and spun was to avoid feeling. It was here that my search for the whole truth and nothing but the truth began. Therapy helped me understand some of these truths, but i wanted resolution and needed to feel the truth in my heart, not just understand it in my head.

After ten years and two kids later, my husband and I divorced. I searched for answers for about two years. I went on a self-discovery journey. I wanted more.

Then I found Michael and my world began to make sense, as well as change everything I knew to be true about my life. Everything that I knew was uprooted, looked at and then resolved.

It took some time to gain the trust of a man who spoke of nothing but the facts about behaviors, belief systems and patterns. It wasn't until later that he modelled the love for himself; Real love - Self-Love!

Waking up and changing my life was not what I had thought it would be. My life went from a controlled experience to a "being" experience. (We will discuss "the controlled experience" at length later in the guide.) Working through this process was the best decision that I have ever made.

Together, Michael and I evolved and expanded this process which we are sharing with you in this guide.

Michael's story:

For me, it began from birth. I was born extremely sensitive and could feel everything in my environment. Both of my parents had been physically emotionally and mentally abused as children. They had done the best to modify what had been done to them but they were still very abusive in their raising of me. My mother had very deep sexual issues and great rage against men. My father was deep-seated with anger and at times had very little patience with me as a young boy. My father's tone and language were often very harsh. My mother's tone and language were often very cruel and cutting. And then there were the times when my mother would take a two-foot wooden spoon and chase me around the house and beat me with it because I had done something to displease her. My household was typically an emotional or verbal battlefield between my mother and my father or me.

The rage, the hate, the cruelty was so intense that I barely felt or remember the love of any kind. I know they had loved me in some way, but I never truly felt it then. It seemed all I could focus on was the darkness that was in my home. I knew from about twelve I wanted out of this house and by fourteen I had begun a plan to leave. I had worked since I was ten and saved money. I had my own telephone and phone bill by the age of fourteen. I bought my first car at fifteen and was saving money to get an apartment. There was no way in hell I was staying with these crazy people any longer than I had to. I played sports and rode my bicycle four miles one way into town everyday to get away from them.

When I was around fifteen years old, I knew intuitively that there was more to life and I wasn't very happy with my childhood or where I was at. My mind would drive me crazy with thoughts and ruminations and yet at other times, I would be calm and centered. This was too erratic and at times, a living hell for me. My internal life had become just like my household. I knew there was something other than what I saw and what I was experiencing.

I don't know how I knew, I just knew in my core that there was something else. And so, my quest began. At first, I delved into psychology, people, their behaviors and the way they saw life. Next I delved into philosophies and religions. And finally, it all came down to me. I had to go within and reflect on my life and who I thought and believed I was.

I had grown up in a middle class blue-collar family. I lived in an average house having average experiences, living with a stay-at-home, emotionally troubled and sometimes abusive mother and a suppressed angry father who owned his own construction business. There was nothing outrageously unique except that we were very "normal" by society's standards. This normal family was filled with mental, emotional, physical and verbally abusive behaviors.

Growing up, I was pressured to go to church and college of which I did neither. At the age of seventeen, I already discovered that neither made any sense and were completely driven by other people's needs or the manipulation of society to make money by forcing young people to go into great debt by attending college. At the time, college was just at the beginning of becoming a new society moneymaker and it was not as important as it has become today nor was it seen as necessary. So, I became an entrepreneur. I started small businesses, some failed, and some succeeded. In my experimental years, I had worked jobs ranging from construction to corporate management. It wasn't until later in life, I realized that all the different types of jobs I had prepared me for what I was about to do as my life's work.

When I started to explore my real life's work and honed in on what it was that made me feel alive, things started to move. I wasn't ignorant of or disregarding what my responsibilities of living in this world involved. I was just experimenting and therefore tried a variety of experiences at least once, enjoying some parts, and other parts, not so much.

I also knew at this time that there was a purpose for my life and that I was to bring something new to the world. A new way of seeing or understanding what has been accepted as normal. This type of knowing is unexplainable. It comes from so deep in your soul that there are no words for and most people don't even believe in it. I have brought with me into this life some great wisdom and it was for me to share with the world to improve the way of living as a human being.

So, as I sought my own inner peace, I tried almost everything in many fields of life, only to discover that no one had put together all of the things necessary in this day and age to acquire your own inner peace permanently. There were many that had great parts, but none with a whole process. Then there were those who had processes, but they all required some sort of sacrifice of self to the process or the person running the process, which made them seem like another religion.

This turned me away. So, I embarked on my own journey applying the things that worked and discarding the things that did not. I became a massage therapist in the 1970s to find a way to heal through the body. I also worked with nutrition and supplementation. I became a certified drug and alcohol family addictions therapist, a hypnotherapist, an energy worker, an intuitive counselor, an ordained minister and certified in at least six more modalities in my search.

In the meantime, I got married at an early age and had four children. During this period, I began advising people intuitively that were usually ten to fifteen years, my elder. As this developed, I realized I had a gift, but my gift had to be refined. Even though I had much intuitive wisdom, there were still many beliefs and programs that distorted my view and understanding of life. It was at this point that my inner search intensified. As I delved deeper, I realized that the dysfunction and abuse from my family created these distorted perceptions I still held.

It was at this point that I committed to myself that I would relentlessly resolve these belief systems and come to a clear, loving understanding of life and myself. The more I delved into my inner process, the further away my wife distanced herself. I loved her with all my heart, but she didn't want to come along. I tried helping her and teaching her what I was learning, but after some time past, she left. It later turned out that the fear of facing her abuse as a child was too much for her.

I went through many jobs and career changes, confrontations with my birth family, distancing myself from my birth family, spiritual journeys, psychological journeys, and working with psychologists in developing new systems and perspectives, delving deeper into the invisible aspects of life and developing a process that brought about complete permanent transformation.

Then I began to share this with others and facilitate them in transforming themselves. During this journey, I worked out the nuances with the aid of those transforming themselves.

Then I met Adele, my love and together we evolved and expanded the process, which leads us to what we are sharing with you in this guide today.

After many trials and tribulations and many many lifetimes of experience, I share with you these wisdoms for you to use or not use as you see fit. I can tell you this, everything here has been tried and used with great success and there is nothing experimental.

There is an answer to everything if you know where to look and how to listen!

With all of my LOVE I gift to you this wisdom, may your life be fulfilled and blessed with your own discoveries of self!

You are who you have been waiting for!

We have told you our stories, now you tell us your story!

Exercise A

Share your story!

_____

_____

_____

_____

_____

_____

_____

_____

_____

_____

_____

_____

_____

_____

_____

What's wrong with me?

NOTHING!

Although it often feels like there is something wrong with you, we assure you that there is nothing wrong with your essence. But like the rest of us, you probably have a lot of dysfunctional belief systems and behavior programs that you would benefit from changing.

When you visit your past, there will be pleasant memories and unpleasant memories. You often see the memories that are pleasant as positive. People often put the memories that are unpleasant in the category of "what's wrong with me.". You carry these memories from your past consciously and unconsciously and they seep through every aspect of your current life.

They are unpleasant because in your mind you have judged them and yourself; in your heart, you know that they are not you!

Along with these memories are what we call blind spots. These blind spots are where the trauma was so great that it damaged or destroyed an aspect of self that no longer remembers what it feels like to be happy or enjoy life. Blind spots are simply aspects of your life that you cannot see or aren't ready to see or bring to the surface.

This very brief summary is why intuitively you may wonder what is wrong with you. Again, we will tell you, **nothing is wrong with your essence**! You are a normal human being who has experienced trauma or abuse of some sort that has damaged your memory of your true joyful self.

- Don't judge yourself if you cannot remember or find the words to write about your past experiences. Don't worry the words/memories will come if you allow them and when the time is right. Everyone is ready in their own time.

- You are briefly visiting your past. You don't have to live there. You don't have to live in those experiences again or re-experience them, you only have to touch on them. You only have to touch on them enough to feel them.

Rest assured that joy and happiness can be reawakened and rediscovered. However, you must commit to recovering that joy and apply all that you know with only one imagined outcome: the reestablishing of your own inner joy and peace.

**Because you are reading this book,
you are obviously SEARCHING FOR your own OZ, something that will lead YOU back to
YOU! Something different than what you are doing right now in your life.**

In order to see and feel things differently in your life, you have to do some inner work. In order to change the trauma, it is necessary to go inward and look at yourself.

This is the "All about you" section.

Remember to stay open! Some of the things that you discover in this guide may go against everything that you felt was real about your abuse. For instance, you may want your abuser to feel your pain or want them to hurt as much as you have been hurt. That's completely normal, but let's put that aside just for a second.

Going inward and how you responded to the trauma or abuse is your key to freedom.

We understand that your experience was traumatic; however, how you respond to or perceive it is the only thing that you can change. The trauma/abuse has already happened and there is nothing you can do to change that fact.

The only thing that you can change…**is how you respond to or perceive it!**

It's All About You

Self-Reflection

Self-reflection is required for your reawakening so that you can understand your trauma. Self-reflection in its purest form is done without judgment.

Because of your trauma, self-reflection is mixed with judgments, core programs, family patterning and beliefs which typically lead the individual to avoid self-reflection. When this occurs the individual usually chooses numbness, busyness, avoidance, distraction, drama or denial in order to avoid self-reflection.

Avoidance often occurs because there is a great misunderstanding that self-reflection leads to self-criticism and self-inflicted pain. There is this conception that self-reflection only brings back the memories and feeling of pain and that the pain must be avoided at all cost and so should the reflection.

Nothing is further from the truth!

Self-reflection doesn't have to lead to self-criticism and self-inflicted pain, but most times it does because of misunderstandings. This is where most people stop growing. It is usually misunderstood because when the memories begin to arise, all of the self-judgments come forth. The typical ego/personality of the individual seeks to avoid these judgments because it is perceived that the judgments only add to the pain, suffering and abuse.

It is actually the complete opposite. Self-reflection leads to self-discovery and eventually, to the elimination of self-judgment, which is the only way to permanent self-transformation.

Michael: For instance, I would like to compare this to an accident where you break an arm and it has to be reset. If you avoid the reset to avoid the pain, it will heal inappropriately or will be crooked. But if you reset it, there will be pain at first, then there will be the appropriate healing and the bone is straight.

Self-reflection is the reset, the straightening out.

Do not let your misunderstanding of pain prevent you from your own reset!

Self-discovery

Self-discovery sounds really healthy, but when discovering something about yourself that you judge, are afraid of or are not ready to face, it can turn sour pretty quickly.

Adele: For example, most people who have been sexually abused have either deprived themselves of the basic need for touch or the true meaning of touch and intimacy or they have gone in the complete opposite direction of over indulgence. This is due to their trauma and understandably so.

Most struggle with loving their bodies and being loved. Many feel the same about other people's bodies, skin close to theirs or the feeling of intimacy. So, if it happened to you young in life, then when self-discovery of your sexuality as a teen and young adult begins to naturally awaken, it can become quite frightening, avoided and/or not pleasant.

If you were emotionally, verbally and/or mentally abused as a young child, you typically have great trust issues with other people because the people who were supposed to love you betrayed your heart. So, as you reach an age where you are to become social, it may become very difficult to be 'normal' because you do not trust others and there is a perception that you must protect, hide or guard your heart.

Sometimes there are people who do the complete opposite. They give themselves away completely sexually and emotionally in order to have the illusion of being loved. This is often in an attempt to avoid the memories of the abuse and convince themselves that they are desirable and loveable.

Coping

Coping can be exhausting as an adult but as a child it simply helped you to survive. Let us explain.

Self-discovery, like self-reflection, is required for permanent transformation. We mentioned permanent healing earlier and want to address this here: Healing/transformation is often considered to have occured when the individual can cope with and learn to live with the trauma. But coping here is only one step on the path to permanent freedom trauma.

Coping is about managing and avoiding your true feelings either temporarily or permanently. They can be exhausting as an adult but as a child they simply helped you to survive.

Here are some examples of what coping can look like as a child:

- A child stays out of their abusers way
- Develops caretaking skills to look after the other kids - winning over their abuser being a good little girl or boy
- Learns to be self-sufficient in the family unit, attempting to control the world around them to feel .
- Doing for others at the expense of self

In these examples the child manages and also avoids their true hurt feelings - that their abuser/parent only shows their appreciation/loves them if the child care takes and is a good little girl or boy, making the parents job easier.

All coping, is simply behaviors and all behaviors are patterns of belief systems. Coping behaviors are simply the display of these beliefs systems. So, using the above examples, if the child believes that they must be a good little girl or boy to get their parents' love and approval, they will act out these beliefs using coping skills such as those described above. Coping is simply belief systems acted out. It has no reality other than other than being acted out to achieve an outcome.

Although coping is often a common step for most people who are trying to transform their trauma/abuse, permanent transformation can take place without coping in individuals who are committed to their own journey. Coping is not bad or wrong-it is just not really necessary. You don't have to settle for coping or comfortably living with trauma.

We have found that there **is** such a thing as the:

<u>Permanent elimination of wounding and traumas as well as</u>
<u>the adverse feelings and behaviors that go along with them.</u>

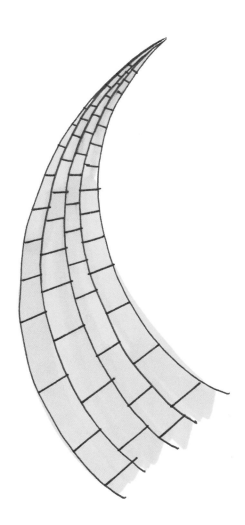

Chapter One
SUMMARY

- **Seven Steps to Freedom (1):** Knowing that you are unhappy where you are and having the desire to change.

- An abuse occurs and then it is over, but what lives on? What lives on is the perceived feeling that is attached to it. If you revisit the experience, it's in the past. Right? The trauma or traumatic memory is what you revisit. I know this is an obvious statement, but it is important.

- The traumatic memory is the thing that has continued and has most likely been affecting your life. The pictures, the sounds, the tactile or sensory memories are the things that linger on and creep into your life and often times disrupt the flow.

- The act of the abuse is a fact, but the perceptions of what occurred and of what you believe are true are the things that will haunt you and affect your life.

- There is nothing wrong with you. No need to judge yourself for not being able to remember your past. You are briefly visiting your past. You don't have to live there.

- Self-reflection and self-discovery create the doorway to transformation.

- Coping is about managing and avoiding your true feelings either temporarily or permanently. They can be exhausting as an adult but as a child they simply helped you to survive.

- **Exercise A** - We recommend that you continue writing your story throughout this entire process.

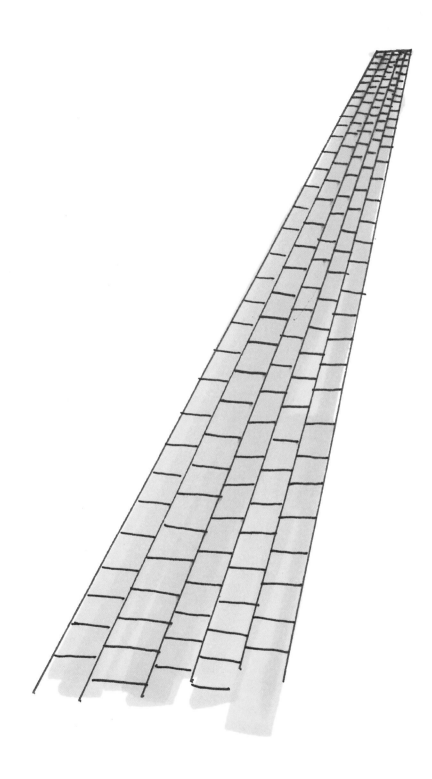

Chapter Two

Sometimes You Just Have to Look into Your Own Crystal Ball to Find Your Answers

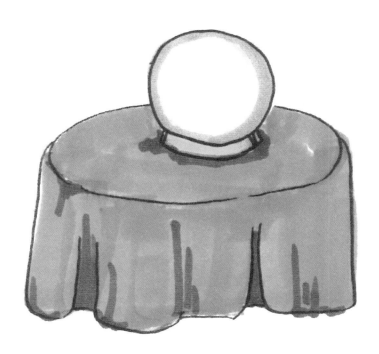

Adele: I avoided this for YEARS!

I hid from my own self reflection, such as, feelings, challenges, shortcomings and secrets for as long as I can remember. And then at 33 years old, I woke up! I came to the realization that it took more effort and energy to hid it rather than to look at it.

Over the years, I have observed the changes in me from this process, as well as witnessing Michael's modeling - this atypical refusal to hold on to anything that was not Love. As he modelled this self-love and the freedom that came with it, I started to become more comfortable with admitting the truth about what I was feeling, perceiving and more importantly, hiding.

The **second step** to Freedom!

Seven Steps to Freedom (2)

Awareness of what makes you unhappy.

Exercise B

What are the three biggest things in your life that make you feel unhappy?

1. _____

_____

2. _____

_____

3. _____

_____

The list that you have identified as things that make you unhappy is most likely what is still affecting you in some way. Your current unhappiness is a result of your traumas and the residual memories of hurts.

We now will share with you many of the concepts that are found in the book, "The 55 Concepts" by Michael. These concepts will provide you with ways to make it easier for you as you go through this process. Theses concepts are meant to be used again and again.

Reflections of Self

Reflections are what you see when you look in to something like a crystal ball or mirror and you see yourself in something else.

Most times your reflections of self come when you are with another person. Whenever you look at someone and judge them you know you have seen your reflection. this reflection is something that you do, have done or think about and consciously or unconsciously judge yourself for.

Concept #1

What bothers you about others, you do now, have done, think about, or believe - **Michael Cavallaro**

Remember what bothers you about others, you do now, have done, think about, or believe. We tend to blame our negative experiences on others or on their actions. But the truth is that it has nothing to do with others. All your discomfort stems from your own beliefs, perceptions and issues. Nothing can bother you that isn't your issue. this is ALWAYS true.

You will feel it because it resonates with you and you unconsciously attach to it. It's the same whether you act on what you are attached to or just think about it: you have connected to it and invisibly made it yours.

Adele: This concept BOTHERED me every time I heard it. It really did. I was so busy judging what I was seeing about others that I never even considered the fact that I was only judging things that I did, had done, thought about or believed.

For example, when I would see someone being taken advantage of, it would bother me. I would immediately defend or try to rescue the person being taken advantage of.

I was simply attached to the unfairness of being taken advantage of myself.

Because of my past experience with sexual abuse, when I would see someone being taking advantage of, I wanted to save them. But in fact, I really wanted to save ME! It was my mirror of what happened to me.

Exercise C

Take the time to go back and look at your list of things that you are unhappy with in your life and answer these questions.

1. Identify something that bothers you.

_____

_____

2. Where do you do, have done or have thought about some version of that in your own life?

_____

_____

Concept #2

People are like mirrors; they reflect your beliefs back to you – **Michael Cavallaro**

You project your view of the world onto others and they become like movie screens that you are watching. In most cases, you don't even realize that you are the movie projector, your beliefs are the film, your experience is the electricity that charges the projector and other people are the screens on which you are watching the movie. Your beliefs are a result of your past. So, every time you see a mirror or judge something, keep in mind it is because you have experienced something like it before and are now projecting the judgment of it onto what you are currently experiencing. In other words, your past has become your present and it will feel familiar. This will distort what is happening in the now moment.

If you look at every person as your teacher, life becomes a learning experience. Look carefully to see what others have brought you to learn, and life will be a growth process rather than a difficult task. There is always something to learn from others, whether you like what they have brought you or not. If you accept their gifts, you will find them enjoyable, if you deny their gifts, you will become judgmental and critical. Remember that it's often what we don't like that we grow from the most. It's common for people to grow only if pushed. Discomfort or being pushed is what often pushes people to grow beyond the norm or status quo.

When you are encountering an experience that is unpleasant, remember always to ask these questions:

- What is the reflection of myself in this situation?
- What has this person brought me to learn about myself?
- Why have I brought this person to me in this way?
- What is it that I am to learn?

Whether you like what they have brought or not, it is to your benefit to look into it and receive the information and gain the wisdom.

Remember it is only unpleasant because you perceive it as unpleasant. What you tend to deny or not see is often what you need to learn the most.

And if these types of people or behaviors keep recurring in your life, it should be evident to you that you have not yet gained the wisdom of something, so look closely to find it. These are good markers for you to make your life easier. In truth, at this moment no one is doing anything to you; it is what you are doing to yourself. This may be tough to hear or understand at first so please be patient.

Adele: From my previous example on concept #1, regarding the fact that I was bothered by people being taken advantage of – in reality, the fact that it bothered me had nothing to do with the person that I was trying to save or rescue.

It bothered me simply because they were holding up the mirror of me - my six-year-old self and my fourteen-year old self who allowed themselves to be taken advantage of.

What I used to see were the people holding up a mirror, and then blaming them for, bringing up something that bothered me, to my attention. Because what was in the mirror was too painful to see, because I was judging myself for having done those things. Until I saw myself in the mirror, I was unable to understand these two concepts.

Exercise D

Go back again and look at that same list of things that you are unhappy with and answer these questions.

1. Identify the multiple mirrors in your life.

_____

_____

2. What are they reflecting back to you?

_____

_____

3. How are you judging yourself?

_____

_____

Judgments

Judgment is a common part of life.

Judgment is often more intense as part of the fallout from being traumatized/abused. Someone who has experienced trauma has judged themselves and/or their abuser in many ways, such as feeling guilty or bad, seeing their abuser as evil or judging their parents for allowing this to happen.

All judgments come from your past experiences and for the most part, are formed when you are young. Even though you are older, these judgments are still with you, whether you think so or not. Although your outlook may be different now, you are still judging almost everything through the eyes of the child who perceived the original event. It is important to understand this as it often leads to inaccurate and childish judgments. Imagine that your childhood judgments as an adult are as valid as asking a four year old how to determine the circumference of the earth. Pretty silly eh?

Keep in mind: you can only judge that which you have already experienced. Otherwise, you would see the wonder of its newness and it would have no meaning.

Exercise E

Name three judgments that you made about yourself as a child, even if they sound childish.

1. _____

_____

2. _____

_____

3. _____

_____

It is almost impossible not to feel some sort of judgement regarding your trauma. What we are about to tell you about judgment might go against everything you have ever believed about judgment. We encourage you to listen with an open mind as this may challenge your logic and current way of seeing things.

And don't JUDGE what we are about to say. Ha!

Because you judge yourself from an trauma/abuse, you may also put those judgements on other people. As a result of your abuse, you often judge yourself. Once you start judging yourself, you will also judge others as well. Often times with trauma/abuse, the person we judge the most is ourselves.

Most times you see things in yourself and then judge those same things in others. It may be in deed or in thought, either in the past or in the present, but you have participated in it at some time.

To see it, judge it or recognize it is to claim ownership of it. To judge something or someone is to say, "I am that which I judge."

Judgments of self

If you feel good or bad about something, it's a judgment.

If there is no feeling, it's an observation, indifference or denial; you should determine which it is if you want life to be easier. It's exhausting when you hold a judgment on someone. Just feel it in your body when you are judging someone. If you do judge, remember that you are judging yourself, because others are your mirrors. Until you cease judging yourself, you will not be able to cease judging others no ifs, ands or buts about this one!

Concept #3

Be an Observer, not a judge – **Michael Cavallaro**

Judgment or observation, it's your choice. If you feel good or bad about something, it's a judgment. If there is no feeling, it's an observation, indifference or denial; you must determine which it is. Remember that of these choices, observation is the most beneficial and a higher aspect of being human. They all look so similar that you may need help in their identification.

Observe: to watch or take notice.
Judge: to criticize, form an opinion or pass sentence
Indifference: the trait of seeming calm, not caring or seeming not bothered by something.
Denial: the act of asserting something that is not true.

Observe things in life. Then choose to participate or not. You are here for the experience.

Behaviors

Adele: The reason why I did not want to admit what happened to me when I was young was simply that I judged my behaviors. I believed that I was my behaviors, when in fact I was not. I AM not!

Concept #4

You are not your behaviors – **Michael Cavallaro**

You often determine who you are by your behaviors. From early on, others judge and approve or disapprove of you based on your behaviors. You may have been told you were bad or good. You may have heard or felt approved or disapproved of because of how you were acting.
For example, a young girl running around a restaurant may be told she is bad or that she misbehaved, which tells her that she is not accepted as she is.

But behaviors are simply actions you choose to take based on your beliefs. They do not define your essence, which is who you truly are. Behaviors can be changed, but you cannot change who you are (your essence). You can choose to be mean or kind, but you cannot choose to be a human or a fish. You are a human, but most of all you are a spiritual being in human form.

Most of the time we judge our behaviors, perceiving ourselves as broken. Believing that you are broken stops any chance of change. If you <u>believe</u> that any part of you is less than or unworthy, there is no way it can be changed. This is self-judgment and self-limiting.

You may be dysfunctional but you are **not** broken!

Judgment of any kind is the source of all pain.

Adele: Because I was checked out (was not present), I fell behind in school. By the fifth grade, I perceived myself as stupid. I didn't just believe that there was something wrong with my brain, I knew that I was completely stupid.

I also believed that I was stupid because I allowed myself to be taken advantage of, and so on. This behavior continued to repeat itself throughout my entire life.

Michael: When you are in this belief system of "I am broken" or "I am stupid," there is no way that you could have considered the possibility that your brain may not have been exercised or your neuro-pathways were not developed because a trauma froze the development that was needed during that time.

Unless there is physical damage to your brain, you are not broken, you are dysfunctional. This can always be changed or compensated for. And even if you have physical damage to your brain you are not broken.

Adele: Hang in there! There's much more!

Who can I trust?

To the abused person, No One!

When it comes to abuse, there is no such thing as trust.
Just know, trust is non-existent when it comes to those who have been traumatized/abused.

<u>This can be changed!</u>

Positive thinking and trying to convince yourself that you can trust again is impossible --it's truly unrealistic and at best temporary. However, if you apply our process and concepts-- you can begin to understand things in a different way so you can be neutral again and move to a trust with wisdom.

When things are done to an individual that break a trust and/or when these things are said to someone that become a betrayal, it changes the experience for that person forever and it typically forms a belief. The abuse we are speaking of occurs when a human being abuses another human being in any way shape or form or they allow the abuse to take place. These are both also betrayals; therefore, a *human* has broken your trust or betrayed you.

After that, somewhere in your subconscious you never truly trust any human again especially if it has happened early in life.

You may want to trust. But the bottom line is; you consciously or unconsciously believe humans cannot be trusted. This may even include yourself. Because of this belief system that may consciously or unconsciously exist, you will not fully open your heart to any human. Now there is a catch, which is that you are a human. Therefore, often at some level the trust of self has been broken (I do not trust my choices, myself, my judgment etc.).

Because of this belief there is much judgment of self and even some self-abuse. After a person has been abused, there is a danger that they may allow abuse, or even abuse someone else or themselves mentally, emotionally, physically, spiritually or sexually.

<u>Self-abuse is the most overlooked form of abuse</u>
<u>that occurs to someone who has been abused.</u>

- Check the circle of the ones that you have or still are participating in:
    - ○ Self-judgment
    - ○ Self-denial
    - ○ Self-criticism
    - ○ Self-doubt
    - ○ Self-shaming
    - ○ Self-imposed guilt
    - ○ Avoiding intimacy
    - ○ Negative self-talk
    - ○ Depriving partners of intimacy
    - ○ Denying self of joy or pleasure
    - ○ Feeling guilt or shame
    - ○ Cannot receive love or loving acts.
    - ○ Feeling unworthy or unlovable
    - ○ Depriving yourself of intimacy

Well, it's time to STOP participating!

Here's the deal, you cannot just stop if you are human. You have to look at what is driving you to continue these behaviors, how you benefit from the behaviors. Many people do not like the word, "benefit." We benefit from these things when they are driven by a belief system. By keeping these things we support the underlying unhealthy belief system that creates them. This is what we mean by benefit.

Adele: Here is another example, so, let's use my old belief that "I am stupid and less than." I used to put myself in positions, like interrupting, not listening and saying things that didn't relate to the subject of a conversation.

This would often cause the person that I was communicating with to maybe reprimand me, embarrass me in public, be frustrated with or yell at me, causing me to confirm that I am stupid and less than others.

I know how to not interrupt and listen and stay within the construct of a conversation. When I no longer believed that I was stupid and less than others, I was able to stop creating those circumstances.

Today, if I accidently interrupt someone, or not listen or say things that are inappropriate, it doesn't bother me and I certainly never have thoughts that I am stupid or less than, because I know I am not.

Self-abuse

No matter what happened to you, you do not deserve abuse of any kind; especially SELF-ABUSE!

Self Abuse is the trickiest and most damaging of all!

Adele: When I became shockingly aware of my thoughts of self-abuse and the subtle communication that came out of me, I was appalled. It was horrifying.

It took some time to dismantle the beliefs and misperceptions that I had about myself. Actually, it took years. **Be Patient.**

Remember, it took years to CREATE them; therefore,
it may take some time to UNDO them.

Keep Searching to
Find Your Own
Answers

Exercise F

List the ways that you abuse yourself.
(It can be by thought, action, deed or verbal)

_____

_____

_____

_____

_____

_____

Adele: Remember, these are things that you have kept to yourself for many years. It took me a while to understand, feel and truly live freely from pain. Judgment is the reason for your pain.

You can change this!

You can live free of pain!

Be patient!

Be strong!

Use the concepts we taught you earlier as tools to keep yourself sane while you work through this guide.

There will be times when your intuition is SPEAKING really loudly to you!

Listen to it!

Chapter Two
SUMMARY

- **<u>Seven Steps to Freedom (2)</u>** - Awareness of what makes you unhappy

- Self-reflect on what makes you unhappy,

- **<u>Concept #1</u>**: *What bothers you about others, you do now, have done, think about or believe.*

- **<u>Concept #2</u>:** *People are like mirrors; they reflect your beliefs back to you.*

- **<u>Concept #3</u>:** *People are ready in their own time.*

- **<u>Concept #4</u>:** *You are not your behaviors.*

- No matter what happened to you, you do not deserve abuse of any kind, especially SELF-ABUSE.

- **<u>Exercise: B</u>:** Know the things in your life that make you feel unhappy.

- **<u>Exercise C</u>:** Know the things that bother you. Where do you do some version of that in your own life?

- **<u>Exercise D</u>:** Identifying your mirrors and how they are reflected back to you.

- **<u>Exercise E</u>:** Identify the judgments that you made about yourself as a child.

- **<u>Exercise F</u>:** List the ways that you abuse yourself.

Chapter Three

What to do with a Twister

One of the things, that most people do when they have been abused, is avoid revisiting the painful memory of the abuse. Many go to great lengths to avoid the memory. Who wouldn't? We get it.

Some people become twisters outwardly and some spin internally to avoid feeling. Either way it's a form of hiding.

In order to avoid the past, an individual must hide from self. They may choose numbing, spinning, busyness, avoidance, distraction, drama or denial. Some may become argumentative or defensive. There are so many choices out there; ways and places where we can hide.

Drama is a big one that people do to avoid.

Concept #5

Drama avoids reality - **Michael Cavallaro**

Getting caught up in the drama, tragedy or whirlwind of life's activities allows you to avoid the real issues in life. So, does busyness. Busyness is a way of occupying the mind and thereby suppressing memories in the unconscious. You unconsciously stay busy to avoid something that you would rather not deal with. Things you might not want to deal with could be a rebellious teenager, a nagging spouse, the realization that you feel alone, unworthy, undeserving, depressed, your own sense of emptiness or even your taxes. The closer you get to the root of a problem; the more drama comes up in order to avoid and distract you from the problem.

It's really only the experience that you are avoiding and the only reason that you are hiding from the experience is because you are judging it in some way.

Adele: I spent most of my life living in the past or in the future, hiding. I missed out on things that I wanted to create and experience when I was not in the present, internally or externally.

And there are some really fun things to experience and see internally and externally here on earth.

The fear, shame and/or guilt were the emotions that stopped me from experiencing those things. I must not have wanted those creations and experiences bad enough, because I hadn't even tried to eliminate these emotions. I believed that there was no easy way to dismantle these emotion. In fact I believed that emotions were real and permanent, so i really never thought about changing or getting rid of them.

Exercise G

Write the things that tend to make you spin, hide or deny.

1. _____

_____

2. _____

_____

3. _____

_____

What to do when you begin to spin inside

The inner twister of avoidance, hiding and/or denying is when your emotions or thought processes are overactive and/or your focus abilities are underactive.

Typically, this spinning begins because there is an emotional trigger. This emotional trigger could be a memory, someone's words, someone's behaviors, and external stimuli etc.

There is also the possibility that you have been spinning internally
since you were young or even in your mother's womb.

This occurs when there is stress or anxiety from the mother or environment while you are in her womb. This stress can also come from external environment after you are birthed which was filled with dysfunction of some sort. This spinning then creates anxiety within and/or disharmony and dysfunction in your outer world. This spinning also affects the development of the nervous system of your body and in turn affects your brain and emotions.

When the twister arrives and you begin to spin, avoid, hide or deny, whatever you do, don't judge it. Just like a tornado when hot and cold airs collide, wind begins to whirl. Imagine that your mind is the cold air and your emotions are the hot air colliding and creating the funnel that begins the spin, just like a twister.

The laws of physics apply here. There will be times when your mind and your emotions begin to seemingly spin out of control.

Adele: When and if this inner twister occurs, do not worry or panic, it is normal for this to occur during the transformational process. I guarantee you that you will try to control it and shut down your feelings. I have seen it WAY too many times as people have gone through this process. I TOO have tried to control my world when I didn't want to see the truth about my past and present experiences.

When your feelings, emotions and thoughts come in like this, don't act!

Do nothing!

Take a moment and get centered
or have a cup of tea.

Do not jump into the twister, as this will always make things feel worse. Not to mention that if you do, you're bound to make more of a mess; bringing in other people, stirring up the drama and creating situations and experiences that don't need to be there.

When one of Mother Nature's tornadoes touch down on earth, there is always less damage when there isn't anything in its way, right? So, don't put things in its way. Don't say things to your partner that you don't mean just because you are in the middle of a twister. Just shut up and go get centered. Ha!

Believe me, I have been in many emotional twisters while doing this process.

Learn from my experience! They are not fun.

When in doubt, do nothing.

When you are in an inner twister:

Grab a chair and sit your butt down
Focus on your heart
Breathe deeply
Exhale slowly
And leave everyone else alone!

Until the twister begins to slow down.
Feel YOURSELF

This Inner tornado typically occurs because your unconscious feelings are rising to the surface and your mind is beginning to react to the memories, thoughts and judgments. When the feelings arise you will want to spin or suppress them, yet at the same time your mind begins to respond and think about it, this creates conflict within you. It will distort your perceptions and the accuracy of how you interpret what you are experiencing at any given moment. This will then lead to blurred realities and often a lot of problems if you start to act on these perceptions.

Stop, Look and Feel!

If you stop, look and feel what is happening, you will begin to become aware of what drives you in these moments. Becoming aware of what is happening to you consciously and unconsciously is a major step in your recovery and the elimination of unwanted experiences driven by the trauma/abuse. It's a major step in your commitment to yourself and your experiences.

<u>**Awareness of how you feel is the beginning of your healing and transformation**</u>

You have to become conscious of what is occurring inside of you.

It is the only way to your permanent freedom. The twister is quite common and is nothing to fear. In fact, the twister can only spin if you are in fear. You have the ability, even if you don't believe it, to slow it down and even stop it. This spinning often continues until much of your shame, fear and guilt are permanently relieved.

Remember, the goal here is <u>not to control this twister</u> - that would be managing or coping. When you are going through this process of transformation, you want to consciously understand and feel what is going on. The key is to experience what is happening consciously not control it! Most people live a controlled experience.

What is a Controlled Experience?

Michael: A controlled experience is what most people use to create a perceived safe experience.

A safe experience is an experience where you don't feel anything other than what you know or want to feel.

Adele: I felt very <u>safe </u>interacting with the opposite sex as long as I could <u>control the experience.</u>

Michael: In a controlled experience, there is nothing new; everything is familiar, good or bad. You know how to handle it and you know what to expect. You know what you'll feel. You know what you'll do. You know pretty much the outcomes and that there will not be any surprising feelings.

<u>There won't be anything unusual; therefore, you will be comfortable.</u>

<u>A controlled experience is an experience where you numb yourself.</u>

A controlled experience is when you're doing things to control things and this is true. It is where you are trying to control an outside experience with the main purpose of controlling what you feel. In this type of controlled experience the individual is trying to create circumstances and experiences that will allow them to feel only that which they know and/or prefer. It is actually a form of denial, the denial of feelings. It is also a form of numbing and becoming unconscious. It is a way to repeat only that which is known and an attempt to obtain predictable outcomes, feelings and results as a form of a fear-based attempt to keep you safe.

Adele: Holy crap, Michael that was a mouth full.

Michael: Yes, that was, wasn't it? It is the same in your life if you do everything that you know repetitively and become a creature of habit. You are controlling your world. People become creatures of habit to create a controlled experience so that they know exactly what's going to happen and can feel safe in their experience. They remove the potential to experience or do anything new because they have a great fear. A controlled experience allows them to maintain the illusion of being safe. This also allows them to be unconscious and live on autopilot.

Doing something new, taking risks or doing things when you don't know what is going to happen, freaks these people out. By doing something new, they might have to actually feel and be alive and the thought of this often terrifies them.

Creatures of habit become numb to their life and are no longer feeling. Yet they appear to be feeling in their circle of life. But what is that feeling? That feeling is a habit pattern! They know where to go, what to do, how to speak and how to look. They have the right expressions, the right looks, the right eyeball roll, the right mouth openings, the right tone in order to create the experience they are looking for. In the beginning, it takes conscious effort but after a while it is all done unconsciously and without thought.

They know how to do all those things and they are habitual - this is a controlled life. He who lives a controlled life lives a dead life; a dead life without new or sometimes any sensation. Even though there may be movement in life, there is no new sensation or experience, this is a predictable life. The life they live eventually becomes dull, familiar and even boring. They will then blame it on their circumstances or partners for not stimulating them. This is simply a projection in order to avoid their denial of their fear and living a controlled life.

Some people mistake the feelings of a controlled life as being alive, but the truth is they are basically automatons that are operating in the human existence, using habit patterns to control their experience and pretend they are "alive".

The controlled experience appears to be a feeling experience but this is due to the programming and the automatic pilot that says you feel this when you do that, or you do this you then feel that, so it is all responsive to a controlled response mechanism and program. It appears to have life. Yet it does not have life.

I am bringing this up at this time so that you can begin to recognize where you are still living unconsciously in order to avoid your fears, beliefs or judgments that deaden your life experience. Ultimately, living a controlled life is like living life as a zombie. You go around do things on autopilot yet there is no real joy, feeling or freedom.

One of the reasons people live a controlled life in relation to this guide is that allows them to believe they are coping with their pain. The problem with this is that they are only covering their pain in a form of denial or numbness by living on autopilot.

I know this first hand. When I was a wounded human being, I tried to protect my heart from further wounds by living a controlled experience. I later discovered that this only kept me numb and that I was getting number the older I got. I wanted a way out. I wanted to feel and "live" again. I had to take the chance of doing new things and placing myself in unfamiliar and uncomfortable circumstances in order to resuscitate my dead life. This is not an easy thing to do. It took great courage and fortitude to go beyond my limited controlled life. But I am so glad that I did it. The work was a bit challenging, but the payoff was magnificent.

When I finally moved beyond the controlled life, I rediscovered the joy of new places and new experiences without the fear. You too can do this. Anyone can do this. But you must want it and be willing to do whatever it takes to bring your joy out and awaken your heart once again. Unfortunately most people are "happy" living a controlled life as it is easier in their eyes than to feel alive and free. There is no disturbance or new feeling so they attempt to patch their controlled experience until one day it all just falls apart and they have no other choice than to wake up.

When you really commit to your awakening and will settle for nothing less, you will find that life starts to have new meaning again and feelings will return. Sometimes you will awaken to a beautiful new life and progressively move forward, while other times you will go through a type of detox. This is where old or suppressed experiences resurface in order to be loved and healed. This stage is often confused as going backwards; We want to alert you that when you reach this stage, if you do, this is not going backwards, it is simply a reawakening of feeling and a sign you are on the right path. It sometimes feels as if you are lost in the past again but we would remind you that you are not lost in the past, you are simply having a life review.

I myself have had many life reviews on my journey. Many were amazing to revisit, allowing me to see what I had never seen before, while others seemed extremely painful, as if I was in them again. The ones that felt painful were when I believed I was back in the past. The ones that were amazing to revisit allowed me to discover things about myself and my life as an observer, knowing that I was not in the past, only reviewing. So, if you find yourself in a life review remind yourself: "this is only a life review, and this will pass".

Rumination

Rumination is repetitively going over a thought or a problem without completion or end.

Let's take a look at why you would ruminate.

Why would you repeat things over and over in your mind? It's annoying, right?
Why people do ruminate? Lots of reasons. You may start ruminating to avoid a feeling that youperceive

as hurtful, fearful, gross, painful etc. Know that you may ruminate about something completely different than the feelings that you are trying to avoid; things such as drama, organization, work, school, family, relationships etc.

Pay close attention to why you are ruminating. Are you trying to avoid something? What are you trying to avoid? Are you enjoying the feeling of the topic or is it giving you this distorted sense of pleasure? If you didn't truly enjoy it, you wouldn't do it. So, it serves some purpose.

Typically, anytime that you are ruminating over something that makes no sense, it is because it is based in the subconscious and is part of a core program or belief system that you are unaware of. So in order to change it you must become conscious of it or let it go if you can.

This is what makes it so difficult to get rid of, but we assure you, by using some of the processes we have developed and others that might exist somewhere on the planet, you can get rid of those running thoughts.

The question is: Do you have the courage to look within and begin your journey of self-discovery?

Many people are afraid to look within because of what they believe they will see and often what they are afraid they are going to see or what they are hiding or denying. This is where the denial program comes in to play.

We want to assure you that this is merely your denial program in action that is supporting the self-abuse program, the not good enough program, and the desire program.

Again, the question is, do you have the courage to discover who you really are beyond these limiting beliefs, beyond all of your judgments and concepts that you have about yourself.

Many people are afraid to do this.

Are you?

Rumination and Storytelling

Rumination- is the repeated focused attention on the symptoms of one's distress, and on its possible causes and consequences, as opposed to its solutions.

Storytelling - making up a story about anything without complete facts in order to fulfill a belief or belief system so that one can justify or explain an experience.

Rumination and storytelling are all about the mind and beliefs. The mind uses these things to distract you from truth and to keep you in the belief system and patterning - so do worrying, fear, guilt, sadness, happiness and more. The stories and rumination create a form of self hypnosis and make the experience feel real and at its peak larger than life so it is all the person can see or feel.

Rumination could even be about something happy. Let us explain! If you are repeating a positive, happy memory over and over again, you are not living in the present. You are in the past and making it feel real in the present, thereby creating a false reality. This process is about looking at both negative AND POSITIVE.

Adele: This was my M.O. - mode of operating, Modus Operandi - whatever! I loved going to places in my mind that made me feel good. You could say it was my happy place for coping with all my sad places. Each time I dismantled one of my sad places, being present became much easier and more enjoyable. I rarely go there anymore except to tell a story from the past, but to be honest with you, I'd much rather spend my time in the present brainstorming on my original thoughts and feelings to create something new.

Happy Moments

If you are seeking positive or happy moments in your life and even holding on to something positive that happened in the past to you to make you feel better, it will cause some challenges.

Adele: Reenacting a happy moment again and again in your mind – a first kiss or a soccer goal that won the game. This is still considered rumination. Why reenact a first kiss in your mind? Why not kiss your partner like that AGAIN and AGAIN, like the first time! Ha!

Michael: Ya got that right, Love!

Holding onto those happy moments in your life means
that you don't believe that you have that peace and happiness
within yourself at this present moment.

That somewhere you believe you must hold onto the past in order
to experience and appreciate happiness in the moment.

This is a false belief!

You simply are chasing something that you believe you do not have.

Many people ruminate, meaning they run things over in their mind, endlessly looping the same thoughts, ideas or reviewing the past or future.

Rumination is typically about the past although it can be done about the future. Rumination is addicting. Why, you might ask?

Because it triggers the stuff that you have suppressed such as self-limitation, unfulfilled desires, and self-justification, just to name a few reasons.

Let's face it! Anything addicting is a pain in the ass. You are a slave to it. It feels like it <u>controls you.</u> Being a slave to anything is not freedom. This what this guide is about – finding your Freedom! Isn't life about free will and choices?

<u>Now this is where it gets tricky.</u>

Rumination is an attachment to a feeling. There is a feeling that you get when you run things over in your mind and consistently replay an event or an experience or a potential experience. This feeling then becomes addictive. It may often feel painfully pleasurable.

Typically, most feelings during rumination are about some sort of painful, unpleasant experiences, which stimulate the memory and feeling of that unpleasant experience. It can be anywhere from uncomfortable or self -judgment to a tragic event.

There is a program somewhere inside of you that says, "This pain is comfortable."
I know this may not make much sense to your logical mind because who would want to feel pain?! But if it wasn't serving you in some way, either consciously or unconsciously, you wouldn't be doing it.

Now it is more complex than this, and you will learn more later in the guide about how things like rumination allow you to continue to have the feeling that supports <u>a belief system</u> that is typically unconscious. This belief system tells you that you deserve to suffer, you deserve pain, you do not deserve happiness or fulfillment or whatever version you are carrying.

Rumination can only be stopped when you discover why on some level you may not be aware of the fact that you feel comfortable with this suffering. Again, it doesn't sound logical and some of you might argue with that, but we still suggest that you look more closely at this and see where, within you, you sort of are comfortable with this suffering?

- It's familiar
- It's painful
- It's disturbing

No matter how you look at it, there is some sort of unhealthy pleasure to ruminating.

It's sort of like people who like to pull the scabs off their wounds or wiggle their teeth when they are loose and feel the pain that comes from wiggling. It isn't exactly that, but that is the closest we can use as an example right now.

Understand that your rumination is all about the re-stimulation of a feeling that you desire on some level.

The rumination on a specific topic, event or experience allows feelings to continue and there is a part of the ego/personality, typically in the subconscious, that feels comfortable with this pain and suffering or this feeling of pain and suffering.

There is a part of your subconscious programming that desires to re-experience the pain or the pleasure/pain feeling.

First, you ruminate because there is a desire. The desire fulfills the subconscious need to self–limit, self-abuse and then it creates a feeling that sustains the pattern. These belief systems make no sense to the logical mind, yet they do exist.

In other words, this pleasure/pain concept is what attributes to some self-abusing. That is really all you have to know for right now.

Shame, Guilt and Fear are temporary emotions based on judgments of your past

Dig deep and find the courage within.

Step into the eye of the twister and observe it. In the eye of the storm is your stillness. In this stillness is your wisdom. This will allow you to become conscious of what is going on. Avoid stepping into the whirlwind of the mind and allowing it to scatter you in your emotions and memories.

This is typically difficult at first but with practice you will master this step and that will allow you to continue on the path of your transformation. The twister is the state of unconsciousness. The more you spin the more unconscious you become and the more destructive the twister is. Becoming aware of how you feel inside and how you got to this place is the awakening of your consciousness. Dig deep and find the courage to become conscious so that you can change all that does not work for you any longer.

Consciousness Cures Everything

The Living Dead – twister free drama avoids reality

Michael: Some people do the opposite of the twister and become living zombies. They withdraw and become disconnected from the world by becoming silent and isolated. They become so still and invisible that they are hardly seen. This is usually done from the perspective of "if I am invisible no one will see me and if they do not see me they will not hurt me." So, you can see avoidance and drama can appear in many different forms.

Which are you?
The Living Dead (one who withdraws) or the Twister?!

Don't take the zombie thing personally, we all go through these stages and I was just lightening things up a bit. We do have to learn to play during this process and not be soooo serious.

Some have said that when one unleashes the realities of trauma, it opens up a funnel for many other things to be released that one might not be ready for. This can be true. However, if you use the tools in this guide and whatever additional professional assistance you are receiving, you will be prepared to do whatever it takes. The truth is that there is a part of you that will not allow an experience that you are not ready for to happen.

You must have committed to yourself to <u>do whatever it takes</u> to be free from these traumas. This internal commitment is absolutely required to be permanently free of them. If you are only half committed, you will only experience half freedom or less.

Yes, there will be difficult and challenging times, but you will be able to free yourself from having to carry these traumas around for the rest of your life.

No matter if you are a crazed spinning mental twister or an unconscious zombie, your realities will tend to get blurry.

Blurred realities

When you are unclear and not centered, your realities start to blur, it will take a toll on your current life.

Michael: What this means is that when the traumas of the past are unresolved, they will bleed into your current day life and act as filters through which you look at life.

When you look at life through these filters, it will distort your current reality. These filters will create a sense and feeling that is not actually happening in your current day experience. These feelings will feel real and you will often interpret these feelings as accurate and real.

By not questioning these feelings and the accuracy of your interpretations, you will begin to blend one situation into another, mixing and overlaying current relationships with those from the past, thereby experiencing things that are actually not real yet you will feel them as real.

Adele: For example, as a result of keeping my secret about sexual abuse and not admitting that I was hurt and not taking care of that distorted situation, I would often place an overlay on my relationships, setting myself up with the belief that my partner would hurt me.

In other words, my current relationships were overlaid by my past experiences, which is not at all fair for the partner who is inaccurately being perceived. Don't worry, there is a section on The Forgotten Partner!

Michael: I wrote that section!

Question everything that you feel. Discern if what you are feeling is accurate.

Concept #6

*Logical, Reasonable and Rational - **Michael Cavallaro***

One of the ways to discern if your feelings are accurate is to determine if they are:
- logical
- reasonable
- and rational

If what you're feeling is not logical, reasonable or rational, then it's not real and is based on a judgment, experience or emotion. Thus, the feeling is not about the present. In a way, it's artificial and based on the past. This ultimately makes the feeling false and inaccurate about what's really going on in the present. Even if the feeling is strong, it's still inaccurate. When you are at this point, it's best to reassess the current situation and look within to find the real source of this feeling. This will assist in avoiding the perpetuation of unconscious programs and creating false experiences. Refer to the following definitions to find out if what you are feeling really is logical, reasonable and rational.

***Logical** - based on known statements or events or conditions.[1] Sensible and based on facts: based on facts, clear rational thought, and sensible reasoning.[2]*

***Reasonable** - not excessive or extreme.[3] In accord with common sense; acceptable and according to common sense.[4]*

***Rational** - having its source in or being guided by the intellect.[5] In accordance with reason and logic; governed by, or showing evidence of, clear and sensible thinking and judgment, based on reason rather than emotion or prejudice.*

Adele: After my experience with the sexual abuse, the words "logical", "reasonable" and "rational" went right out the window. I had to look at the fact that I believed that men in an authority position would eventually hurt me. I also had to admit that I believed that almost every thirty-something man's intention was to take advantage of young teens. I also believed that almost every young male teenager was interested in touching small children inappropriately.

And finally, I had to look at the fact that I believed that every "touch" meant "sex." Touch was not caring, loving or sensual. Nope. For me, touch was not safe. It was creepy, dirty, gross and sexual.

This last one was big for me and it sucked. This was one of the reasons that I kept searching for the freedom that I spoke of earlier. I wanted to be free from this. I wanted to be normal when it came to being sexual. I wanted touch to be relaxing and enjoyable, not be anxious every time someone touched me.

Why couldn't I enjoy touch?
Why did I have to be robbed of the enjoyment of touch?

NOT FAIR!

I know, I made that sound a little emotional, but it was emotional going through it.

There was anger, sadness, disappointment and blame!

Knowing what I know now, and the peace I feel inside of me regarding "touch" makes me so very grateful that I kept searching.

You see, when you have all these misperceptions, you tend to blur realities and mix things up--even when you're absolutely sure that what you are seeing and feeling appears correct.

You truly must learn to <u>question everything</u>.
In other words, question your thoughts, feelings and actions and what you are perceiving.

When you're in this blurred reality state, which is most of the time during your transformational process, you often can't see straight. Your current reality is so distorted because of the trauma that you don't even know you are living in a blurred reality.

You are so convinced that what you are seeing and feeling is true, that you find it almost impossible to believe that you could be misperceiving. Again, **when in doubt, do nothing.** Accepting this is quite difficult at first for many. But once you do, you begin to discern the difference between fact and what we will call "trauma fiction" and you begin to see and feel differently.

It requires a certain amount of commitment to yourself to write down or record all the debris from your trauma/abuse that is swirling around in your life currently? Fortitude is imperative during this process. Writing it, is important. It helps you release and process. Most people avoid the writing part. This is the beginning of your freedom.

Write or record it here and now. Be detailed, factual and honest with yourself. Be committed to your freedom and you shall have it!

Exercise H

What is still swirling around in that mind of yours regarding any traumas or abuse that you may have had?

_____

_____

_____

_____

_____

So, now, you have done some self-reflection and self-discovery and maybe even looked at some self-confessions, as well as some secrets. With that, most likely, come some judgments on self and maybe others. This is when things start to move and become clear that you are traveling a new path, whether you like it or not.

I am not in Kansas Anymore

Suddenly, the reality that you have been living in may not feel the same.

You will sometimes feel that you are not in the same state of mind anymore or for that matter, not in the same state anymore, like in the state of Kansas for Dorothy. Ha!

When you experience this feeling, some desperately choose to run back to the past, the old way of living. We hope that you don't do this and that you keep reading.

If you happen to have this urge of going back to the past in your old way of being, understand that a part of you is looking for the familiar. It has been what you have built your identity upon. And now that you are creating a new experience for yourself, your identity is freaking out.

Sometimes this brings about a deep sense of the loss of identity.

<u>Who will I be if I am not this wounded person?</u>

At times, you may also feel as if you are disassociated from your old life and what you have known up until now. We can assure you this is a common state and a sign that you are moving into a healthier experience.

<u>Many who have been abused have created an identity of "victim."</u>
<u>If you maintain this identity you will never be free</u>

However, it is also very common for people to panic a little bit because they may have built their identity upon being a victim and wounded. Most traumatized/abused people have created some identity like this.

Therefore, when changing from the wounded victim to a healthy sovereign individual, it typically brings up panic and fear. Rest assured the state does not last and you will eventually evolve into the "new you".

We are not asking you to give up your identity of victim immediately. At this time, we are simply preparing you to be "willing" to go from victim to survivor and then beyond. In our classes and individual sessions, there is much support for this loss of identity stage and plenty of material to explain to you why and how this is happening. In other words, there are answers.

<u>There is no problem without a solution!</u>

Waking up

Waking up is when you care more about yourself than you do about how you look or how others perceive you.

Waking up is a wonderful thing as long as you are not judging everything that you are waking up to. When we speak of waking up, we are talking about becoming conscious of, looking at and being honest with everything about you and your surroundings. Basically, becoming conscious and aware of what is true in the now moment.

This is about taking back your life, changing your direction and becoming the creator instead of identifying with the victim role.

The Journey begins

Do you have reasons why you might want to wake up?

<u>Let's think about this a moment. Let's face it.</u>

Why the hell would you want to wake up and pull apart a covered wound?
Why wouldn't you want to just let it lie?
You might be feeling quite fine right now.

We get it.

The problem is with the covered wound is that it is infected. And sometimes the only way to get to the infection is to open it up and cleanse the wound.

For us personally, when those wounds started to affect our relationships, and prevented us from our dreams, goals and creations, we wanted to rip them apart and dig in. We both reached a point, before we met, where the pain and discomfort of the way we were living exceeded our desire to remain unaware. The pain of our behaviors and patterns outweighed the joy in our lives and we came to a crossroads where we decided to change the direction we were moving in. This is basically where most will choose a different path.

<u>Don't wait until the pain of living exceeds the joy in life in order to heal/transform.</u>

Doing it by waiting until you're so miserable and you can't stand it anymore that you have to change will cause a split within you. You have come to the point where you're either going to crack or change. You must choose to live from your heart OR allow your mind, which is suppressing everything, to make you crazy.

Quite often this tipping point is encountered somewhere between the ages of 30 and 55.

For those of you that are in your late teens or in your twenties, we suggest that you consider doing it now. By doing it now, you have less baggage. This means that you have created less of a mess in your life to clean up.

Typically, what happens is that because of your trauma, you make choices and decisions based on the filters and distortions of your belief systems that were caused by the trauma. Making choices through these distorted filters creates additional traumas, misunderstandings and more wounds that have to be transformed.

Well, you don't have to transform those wounds you could also simply live more wounded instead. But we wouldn't advise that.

Exercise I

Write three wounds that are getting in the way of your relationships, dreams, goals or creations.

1. _____

_____

_____

2. _____

_____

_____

3. _____

_____

_____

Trailing back

Digging inward is not just about looking at your behaviors. It's about what's underneath your behaviors. It's about trailing back to what started those behaviors, thoughts and feelings.

We will show you how to trail back in Chapter seven - The Four Building Blocks of Beliefs and Identity.

Really digging in, to the wounded parts requires openness, patience, commitment and determination. In other words, how bad do you want it?

Will you do what it takes and keep going when you want to stop, during your transformation? The two of us were willing to do whatever it took and it's not because we are better than anyone else. It's because we were being selfish. We wanted something. We wanted to live a life that flowed, a trauma-free lifestyle.

Typically, people are taught that being selfish is a bad thing. We would tell you that there are two types of selfishness. The first one is selfish where you are taking at the expense of someone else. The second type of selfishness is where you care for yourself above all else. This self-care is what we like to call healthy selfishness.

Seriously! Have you had enough?

Are you ready for a new direction? Maybe, you want to do something different. If so, awesome choice!

One of the signs that you are truly transformed is when you no longer feel responsible for or affected by others. It is common in our culture to be told and brainwashed that it is your responsibility to take care of other people. We would tell you that this is highly inaccurate. It is like trying to be a lifeguard and you don't know how to swim. Very few people have transformed themselves enough to even swim, let alone save another person.

Everybody on this planet is responsible for their own transformation. This isn't to say that if they need help or coaching you ignore them. No, quite the contrary. You openly with a loving heart help other people but only if they ask. It is not yours to impose your ideas or your recovery on another human being. Like everyone else I myself had to get over this before I could truly move on with my own transformation.

So, here we are, sharing our wisdom with you. This guide outlines our process and what we have personally worked out and have experienced. But that is all it is-- simply an outline of the process. In order to have true freedom, each person will need to gather their own unique patterns and distortions that they have created and transmute them into a greater understanding and dissolve those that no longer serve your journey of awakening.

Remember, you have created all of your experiences and interpretations either consciously or unconsciously and if you have created something, you can also undo it. Knowing this theoretically should be greatly empowering.

We cannot say this enough.

So, know this and keep this in mind:

- You are dismantling all of your distortions that you have created.
- Be patient, determined and follow the process
- If you follow the process (and don't skip any steps) I guarantee you that you will begin to feel the freedom.

Now it begins.

Come prepared for the next chapter to see something new.

It will challenge almost everything that you have been told. It may be the key to your freedom!

<u>You may take this information and use it or disregard it, as you choose.</u>

<u>We do not imply you have to do anything.</u>

<u>We are only sharing a process that has worked for hundreds of people.</u>

Chapter Three
SUMMARY

- Your Inner tornado typically occurs because your unconscious feelings are rising to the surface and your mind is beginning to react to the memories, thoughts and judgments.

- Hiding, denying, avoidance (Inner twister) typically occurs because your unconscious feelings have risen to the surface and your mind is beginning to react to the memories, thoughts, and judgments.

- The Controlled experience is a form of denial, the denial of feelings. It is also a form of numbing and becoming unconscious. It is a way to repeat only that which is known and an attempt to obtain predictable outcomes, feelings and results as a form of a fear-based attempt to keep you safe.

- You may start ruminating to avoid a feeling that you perceive as hurtful, fearful, gross, etc. Know that you may ruminate about something completely different than the feelings that you are trying to avoid; drama, organization. It is merely your denial program in action that is supporting the self-abuse program, the not good enough program, and the desire program.

- **Concept # 5** - *Drama avoids reality*

- **Concept # 6** - *Logical, Reasonable and Rational*

- By not questioning your feelings and the accuracy of your interpretations, you will begin to blend one situation into another, (blurred realities) mixing and overlaying current relationships with those from the past, thereby experiencing things that are actually not real yet you will feel them as real.

- Will you do what it takes and keep going when you want to stop, during your transformation? Really digging in, to the wounded parts requires openness, patience, commitment and determination.

- **Exercise G:** Being aware of the things that make you spin, hide or deny.

- **Exercise H:** Identifying thoughts that are still swirling around in your mind about your trauma.

- **Exercise I:** Wounds that are getting in your way of your relationships, dreams, goals and creations.

Chapter Four

The Mind

Brian (Brain)

An Understanding of your Thoughts, Feelings, Behaviors and Belief Systems

Understanding the background and the depths of you, as a human, will make it much easier for you as you unravel the feelings that have kept you stuck/limited.

This chapter will give you more of an in-depth understanding about your thoughts, feelings, behaviors and beliefs. Now that you are aware of how to cope with a twister, let's look beyond the twister and start to unravel some of the things that have you all twisted up.

<u>We will teach you how to do more than just cope, one step at a time!</u>

<u>Again, be patient with yourself.</u>

<u>Don't judge what you have done in the past, or what you choose to do now.</u>

We just can't say this enough.

This process needs to be absorbed a little at a time!

This process is like a ball of yarn. You need to unravel it carefully and in a timely fashion.

Adele: I would like to share with you what this process looked like from my perspective while I was going through it, from the "ball of yarn" analogy.

The Different Ways People Look at their Pain

- Some acknowledged that there was in fact a big ball of yarn that existed within them (Big ball of yarn = wounds, judgments, unwanted thoughts, feelings, beliefs, behaviors) and then did everything in their power to pretend that it didn't exist.

- Some saw the potential of the yarn and sometimes attempted to unravel it, so that they would one day potentially create something wonderful with the yarn but then got fearful or said it was too much work and stopped.

- Then there were those who unraveled it and continued to observe the unraveling, watched the changes taking place and were quite mesmerized by those changes. They did what it took to see all the yarn in all its beauty. They completely unraveled the yarn, knowing that some parts of the yarn were damaged or frail or maybe worn. Some parts were not useful for creating maybe a blanket and some parts were. They saw the entire ball of yarn as neutral, not good or not bad, but just as it was, that one day they would create something new from their essence and not from the family patterns and soul patterns of yarn that they had been given.

- Some were on the fast track and some were on the slow track; although the speed did not matter because everyone was ready in their own time.

- If you are on the fast track, don't judge others who move at a different pace than you.

- Don't compare yourself to others because each person's process is different.

Concept #7

Everyone is ready in their own time!

Sometimes you may think others should do things because it is so obvious to you. Who are you to know when it is their time? Who are you to say how obvious it is? We do not have the right to make another do it in our time, even if it looks wrong or makes no sense. It may look right for them on the outside, but they may not be internally prepared. Don't worry or focus on others doing their work. This is controlling and judgmental. Focus on yourself and your own timing. You are the only one who truly knows what is right for you, even if you are unconscious of it.

Okay, now that we got that out of the way. Are you ready to learn? Is your time now?

Adele: I would suggest that you go get yourself a cup of tea/coffee/water. Go to a place where you can focus because in the next few pages, there will be lots of information that will be outlined for you. This background information is needed for you to go through the process in chapters seven and eight.

Here we go!

Can You Identify?

Michael: As human beings, we create our personal identity from what we believe we are supposed to be, what we were told about ourselves, how we were treated as children, how we behaved and how other people responded to us. After repeated experiences involving others and our own behaviors, choices and interpretations, we created an identity about ourselves and then believed this identity to be who we are.

Adele: I know, the above paragraph was packed with information. I warned you, didn't I? How's the tea? Ha!

Michael: Alright, alright enough about the tea, Adele! LOL!

Ya want freedom, don't ya?!

Have you made that decision or commitment yet???

Let's get back to that question in a later chapter.

<u>You can decide later whether true freedom is for you, or not.</u>

Example I

Identity turning into Self-Abuse

Adele: When my ex moved in with his girlfriend, my daughters immediately took a liking to her and then eventually started seeing her as a mother figure.

Aaaaaah!

I don't care what anyone says about this subject, being a mom and watching this happen is quite difficult. It's more than difficult. It is a horrible feeling. Most will not admit it.

They are <u>MY</u> children. <u>I AM</u> their mom! What's she gonna teach them?!

<u>No one</u> could take my place! I gave birth to them.

Thoughts above will arise and hit you smack in the face no matter how much work you have done on yourself, simply because of your <u>identity</u>. The <u>identity</u> that is attached to being a mom is a cultural thing that was embedded in there for generations.

The identity is what you believe you are, rather than the role you play.

Playing the role of a mother is the act of mothering. which includes caring for your child physically, emotionally and mentally. They are jobs and things you do, not who you are.

Michael: This <u>identity</u> piece is necessary for you to understand. In a later chapter, we will take you through our Four Building Blocks of Beliefs and Identities.

Adele: Michael! I am telling a story here!

Michael: My apologies, Sweetie. Go on!

Adele: Thank you. :) Those thoughts about - I AM their mom - sound funny to me now, because I don't feel that way at all anymore.

While it was happening, I never would have said, "I am their mom, Lady" out loud, let alone to my daughters. No way! Instead, I kept it a secret. Yes, "being their Mom" was one of my identities but sharing those words with my daughters would have robbed them of the opportunity to have a relationship with their dad's girlfriend.

So, I encouraged them to get along with her and observe, not judge her, well, out loud, that is. I knew that was the right thing to do. I taught them that people were not their behaviors and they needed to be honest with how they felt and not judge someone's behaviors. I also taught them to speak up if it was a behavior that went against their own growth. But at the same time, I kept that secret about my "mom knows best" identity very quiet, <u>still holding on to it internally</u>.

I would continually tune into my daughters' relationship with my ex's girlfriend - when they would express good feelings and not so good feeling about her – and each time they expressed something good about her, my identity would be crushed.

Over the years, I have seen others manipulate their children to make them believe false things about the other parental figure, just to appease their identity. Trust me, I have had thoughts of that very same manipulation, but I just couldn't do it – instead I allowed it to hurt my heart. It hurt my heart that they could possibly love another mother-figure. So, instead of figuring out why, I decided to just feel bad about myself. (Everything that is underlined in this paragraph is self-abuse, folks!)

I questioned whether it made me less of a mom in their eyes. As long as she existed, my identity was threatened. So, I killed her. (Ha!) I am totally kidding! Actually, I ended up really liking her in the end and currently, she is not even with my ex any longer and we all still have a relationship with her.

Example II

Projection of an Identity that was your own.

Adele: My current husband had a child (my step-son) who I looked after part-time. He was eleven. I began to be seen as a mother-figure. Now the shoe was on the other foot. I would have to potentially feel the pain of my current husband's ex. I made a connection with her from the start, thinking that would ease the pain (That was so my MO!) but it was still difficult for her because I was where she stood for twenty years. I had empathized with her, silently, of course.

There was more potential hurt after the arrival of the grandchildren (on my husband's side). My step-daughter wanted to know what the grandchild should call me as a stepmom and I told her, just have them call me, Adele. I didn't want anything to be taken away from my husband's ex. Silly, right? I know.

Even when I eliminated the grandmother title, I had still believed that there was hurt involved in the beginning, but I found out later I was wrong. That was my own projection when it came to the grandchildren. This was a form of self-abusing - worrying obsessively about other people's feelings. She expressed on numerous occasions that she loved how I loved the grandchildren. I guess the grandchildren meant something different for her.

Because of the connection that I made with my husband's ex, I was honored to be by her side with the rest of the family when she died. I Love Her.

There will almost always be hurt involved when it comes to identity.

When I finally dismantled the identity of Mom, I started to have a different relationship with my daughters. I still love them with all my heart, but in a different way. I love their essence. I love what they have become. I love how they feel as I continue to watch their yarn unravel.

I am still a good mom, but my relationship with the two of them has grown into something that I never thought possible -- Mom without all the hurt and crap that goes along with it!

So, moral of this story:

<u>DROP the IDENTITY</u>

There IS a way!

Wait! Don't drop it yet, let us take you through the process first, for goodness sake!

Judgment Day

You typically judge yourself based on the identity that you have created, your behaviors, the values you were taught, the responses of others and what our culture or environment tells us is good or bad.

<u>Basically, you create an identity from what the outside world tells us and/or what you believe it tells you you should be, as well as how the outside world interprets us.</u>

In reality, the judgments you have of yourself are actually someone else's that you believe are yours. Knowing this frees you to stop judging yourself, if you so choose.

Example I:

Still having judgments but respecting another person's space

Adele: The last four years of my mom's life, I found her quite darling. I finally began to truly accept her for who she was. She and I came to an agreement of what we wanted from each other. We dropped the identities of how we saw one another. Well, let's say, she really tried, considering she didn't know this process.

I explained to her that I refused to pretend to have a close relationship with her if she continued to judge who she believed I was and what she thought that I should be. Basically, I would not allow her to run her patterns with me, the way she did all my life. I told her she would have to meet me on my level and drop the petty BS.

She tried as best as she could in my presence. Often times it was, "Oh sorry, Adele, let me start again, don't leave," because she knew that I would leave. She knew that I wasn't bluffing. I was okay with not having her in my life if she chose to continue her patterns with me.

That may sound cold to the average person, but the love that I had for myself was not going to endure the subtle abuse that she sometimes threw my way. At this point, I was not judging her, I was only dealing with her behaviors and patterning. I knew by now that the abuse was simply coming from her own distorted patterns and she wasn't doing it to me, she was doing it for her, because she was stuck in her patterns.

I respected her life; therefore, she needed to respect mine. She learned to do this as I kept her accountable. She learned a lot from me, as I did from her. Often times, she didn't even know how to act when all of us siblings were together. I would watch her going back and forth, trying to decide how to behave.

The couple months before she died, she actually had revealed some of her judgements, guilts, regrets, fears and hurts. A couple months before she died, I assisted her in releasing some of them. She was a powerful being; she just sometimes had forgotten her inner beauty when she lived here on earth.

"A friend is someone who knows the song in your heart and can sing it back to you when you have forgotten the words." C.S. Lewis

I reminded her of her inner greatness, as well as, all the positive human skills that she DID teach me. I Love Her.

Where Do Beliefs and Thoughts Come From?

People are more than their thoughts or what they believe.

YOU are not your thoughts. You are the creators of your thoughts. Your thoughts come from your beliefs. Beliefs eventually turn into belief systems. Beliefs are assumed truths. Things that you experience, perceive and assume to be true or real become your beliefs.

Michael: When I was young, my mother would scream when she didn't get her way. She frequently became frustrated or stressed out. This eventually became a normal way for her to communicate.

For me, this eventually created a belief that when people are stressed or yelling, there is going to be some kind of hell to pay. In this case, the "hell" was that I would be verbally or emotionally abused, and on occasion physically abused.

You see, I had experienced this behavior and result so many times that it became an assumed truth and expectation. I then projected this onto all the rest of the areas of my life.

Whenever someone would get hostile, I knew to expect some sort of "attack" and was always prepared to defend myself. This caused many difficulties in the workplace and in all relationships.

It's All Very Systematic

A belief system is a complex design of multiple beliefs creating an entire interwoven system that you assume to be a reality or truth.

Michael: The experiences you are having and are perceiving to be real are experiences you are creating based on your belief systems and perceiving through your own belief system. Belief systems are what you believe to be true about yourself and your world. This is not to say that two or more people may have the same beliefs. If this is so, it is simply that the two people have the same beliefs due to the way they interpreted their world, not that the beliefs are absolute truths.

<u>The biggest challenge is that people believe that their beliefs are real!</u>

<u>Beliefs that are believed to be real, create realities that are perceived.</u>

<u>What people perceive is a reflection of what they believe.</u>

<u>When you believe your belief, it is real to you and no one else, unless they have the same belief.</u>

In a sense, they are real because they are based on what you have experienced in your life; therefore are real only to you. Keep in mind that just because you have experienced it and it is your truth, it doesn't make it true for everyone, everywhere. This is what we call a relative truth, relative to you and your experience only.

<u>An absolute truth is something that is true for everyone and everywhere all the time.</u>

An example of an absolute truth would be:

- You exist
- There is life
- The advanced laws of physics

We want you to clearly understand:

<u>You are not your thoughts or your behaviors!</u>
<u>You select your thoughts and behaviors, consciously or unconsciously,</u>
<u>based upon your belief system!</u>

Cementing Things in Place

Eventually these beliefs and judgments get cemented in place by growing what are called neural pathways in the brain which can be likened unto an electrical wiring system.

Adele: Okay, that is a good analogy, but I am hoping you don't get all *Einstein* on me, sweetie.

Michael: Well, I will try to keep it brief, and not too *Einstein,* as Adele is saying.

The more the thoughts occur and are repeated, the stronger they become and the more physical these neural pathways become. These neural pathways allow and conduct the frequencies and the thoughts that they were built upon. We don't want to get into too much of the science of this, but this is a very brief explanation.

Continuing with the example of my mother, as the verbal abuse kept coming, the neural pathways in my brain developed into strong energy highways that when activated became stronger and stronger until they became an unconscious way of being and reacting to the yelling. To the point that I would respond to yelling or verbal abuse instantly, without awareness.

It became an autopilot response that I then assumed it to be a "normal" response or way of being. After a while, all I needed was to hear yelling and I would respond, no matter what was actually happening.

After being traumatized and programmed for so long, I could not discern what the yelling was about, and my autopilot was to protect and defend myself without question. And boy, did that make a lot of messes in my life.

Getting Charged

Although you can't see thoughts or feelings, they are real.

Anything that exists has substance even if you can't see it. Thoughts exist as a substance called energy.

While you can't see this energy, it has a charge, much like an electric current.

Later in this guide, you will eventually want to remove the charge of what we call your core programs.

<u>Removing a charge requires you only to touch on the feelings.</u>

You will only be visiting the charges of these core programs. You don't have to live there forever. You are just going to touch on the feelings - Touch long enough to retrieve the belief and connect to discharge it.

Examples:

Adele: Experiencing a charge

1. My daughters come home. "Mommy, we had so much fun with daddy's girlfriend! Aaaaaaah…. my entire body would light up with a envious charge.

2. Watching an older man clearly creeping on a small child. Aaaaaah…my entire body would become enraged.

3. Watching someone (adult or child) being disregarded. Aaaaaaah…my entire body would become angry and step into protective mode.

Your thoughts have a charge and, when repeated, the charge gets stronger, creating energy patterns that affect the neural pathways in the brain and transmit a signal.

This energy pattern eventually becomes the foundation of beliefs if they aren't already supporting an existing belief.

Michael: As a child, I was very sensitive to my environment. I could feel when my house was on the edge and no words were spoken about it. This feeling was a warning that something horrible was about to go down in the house, but you never knew how or exactly when, which created a feeling of always having to be on guard or on alert, even if there didn't appear to be anything happening.

I felt it! I knew something was about to happen! This created anxiety and stress because I was anticipating what would happen when I had this feeling. On the outside, nothing may have happened yet, but boy could I feel it coming. This is just one response/effect that a charge or an energy has on a child or individual.

Our beliefs and thoughts are energy and the energy of each belief or thought has a specific frequency, much like the frequency on a radio. Just like a magnet, these frequencies will attract other frequencies in the form of people, places, things and events. We will then have experiences and interactions where our frequency matches similar frequencies, people, places, things and events.

These frequencies or "energy waves" have different vibrations that create many patterns that weave and overlap forming a complex pattern that we call a matrix, which can sometimes make it difficult to move or make changes in our lives.

When Thoughts Become Behaviors

When a thought is turned into a behavior, it makes it very difficult to change.

This is true because at this point, the belief that was once invisible turns into something physical, a behavior. All your beliefs, thought patterns and frequencies interweave and connect in some way. So, in order to change your beliefs in the thoughts, you have to unwind or untie the knots of these beliefs in order to find the root, or source, where they began so you can make the changes as close to the initial creation of the belief as possible. There are processes which we use to actually shift these beliefs permanently.

Starting to Change

By being aware of the problem, you can at least begin to cope and attempt to consciously change your behaviors.

To permanently change these beliefs, you have to "dig deeper" and ask yourself why you have that belief and where it came from.

<u>You don't just wake up one day and start believing in something.</u>

You have to untie the knots and trail back to where this originated. For instance, in my case, it took me years to untie the knots of sexual abuse. There were many layers. Believing that love meant giving myself away, kept me in the pattern until I was in my thirties.

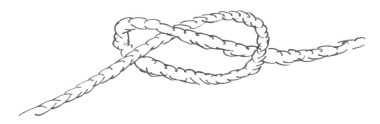

Michael: Once I realized what I did not like feeling and that it was not "normal," I distanced myself from my family at a very young age and started working on myself in order to stop this painful cycle. I remember thinking as a teenager that I had to remove these painful feelings, they were not me and I would not live with them!

I had to stop behaviors and change beliefs and perceptions to do this, which is what you are learning. This then gave me the skills of discernment and being able to handle hostility from others in a whole new way.

So, you could say, that my parents' dysfunction taught me--no, forced me--to change the family patterning and a great many other lessons about life and human patterning.

<u>If you follow this process,</u>
<u>You will be free from your limitations because that's what you deserve.</u>

Getting to the Roots

The root origination of a pattern (meaning where the pattern originated from) must shift for the thinking to shift.

If you cannot get to the memory, you can use the feeling of the belief. This often occurs when the original belief was created prior to cognitive development, usually before the age of three or four. Ultimately the belief/feeling behind the thought must change for the process to permanently change.

The root of any belief is in the feeling of the belief.
This means that feeling creates beliefs (not emotions or thoughts),
then the belief creates thoughts and emotions.
All emotions are based on beliefs!

This is why you must feel to heal. You have to trail back to the feeling behind the thoughts and beliefs. You don't have to dwell on the feeling, but you have to feel it.

Sometimes you may change one pattern or set of thoughts and later do something that looks like the one you just shifted. While these changes are important, **all** connected patterns or the roots of the patterns must change for the thinking to shift permanently.

Simply meaning, you cannot think your way out of this.
Understanding it is not enough.

Sorting It Out

You should imagine your journey as being like a large web of different patterns of your belief system.

This is not a linear process.

This is important to know. Knowing this will eliminate many expectations and disappointments about how you see or experience your progression to transforming/healing.

For example, you may have been able to unravel certain parts of your thoughts and beliefs from your past, and at the same time, there will be parts that you just couldn't face at certain times in your life.

There are many facets of how you and your belief systems are made up. One part of this journey is called sorting. It is where you sort through the different aspects of your beliefs.

<u>In chapter seven, we will take you through the Building Blocks of Beliefs and Identities.</u>

It takes time and patience to sort through the web and discover the root or the core program but it is well worth it.

After you have sorted and found the root/core program, the root of the pattern must be shifted by using the method that we are explaining in this guide or any other valid proven way that works for you.

Much of this may sound or feel overwhelming and complex.

Let us reassure you that it is no different than learning something new. In the beginning, it is often challenging but after some time and experience, it gets easier and easier.

Going from the Head to the Heart

Going from the head to the heart is imperative if you want everlasting, permanent change.

To feel the point of origination will expedite your process, for without feeling, little or no change is possible.

And especially if you want your change to be permanent.

Thinking about it or intellectually knowing about it is never enough to shift the root of any belief!

Concept #8

You Must Feel to Heal – Connecting your heart to your heart - **Michael Cavallaro**

Feeling puts you in touch with your heart. Feeling puts your intellect in touch with your intuition. Feeling is the only way to know what is in your heart or innermost being that needs to be resolved. This type of feeling is sensate, intuitive, you get a vibe, it is sensing. Most people talk about feeling and mean emotions. You feel emotions but they are not real. Emotions are created by your conscious and unconscious beliefs that tell you what emotions you should have.

Learning to feel is different than thinking what you feel. Thinking your feelings avoids that which you do not wish to feel and allows you to believe you are in control. It also allows you to believe that you have resolved the issue so you can stuff it deeper inside, hoping not to feel it. It is a form of avoidance. Most people use this avoidance technique because it tricks the mind into believing the issue is gone.

Victims and tragedy or drama seekers like to emote. It feeds the drama energy, which allows them to avoid the truth and avoid actually seeing the problem. They often use it as an excuse to feel alive or to show they care. Caring is not emoting and emoting is not caring, they are different. Some say they only feel alive when they emote, but this is just a form of adrenaline rush addiction which allows you, yet again, to avoid true intimate feeling. This may sound cold but we assure you that it is not. Lack of emotion does not equal lack of caring; this is a false belief.

Drama does not heal, it entraps; it's a way for the ego to perpetuate its program. Remember drama avoids reality and keeps you in your programs and away from responsibility or ownership of your emotions, behaviors, judgments and creations. Drama and emoting release the steam from the pot temporarily but never solve the problem, which in turn will be experienced again and again.

'Feel to heal' simply means to expose yourself to or witness the experiences that you perceived you felt and accept them unconditionally. You have to feel your feelings in order to heal your feelings and in truth, the healing doesn't really take place.

All that happens is that you allow the old feelings to pass through and out which gives you a resemblance of healing. Its loving back your creations. It's unconditional acceptance of your experiences. It's whatever verbiage you would like to use. But as long as you stay in fear of that which you believe to be your reality, then that is your reality and it's eternal, at least until you decide you want it to be different.

When the head connects with the heart, there is spiritual wisdom on earth. When you truly feel, you know your truth. This sense of knowing is the wisdom of spirit and the soul.

Again, the more often you think the thoughts and the more emotion and feeling that is put into them, the stronger they are and the more difficult they are to change. These are the secrets of being human that no one speaks of or maybe no one knows.

Most likely being in your thoughts is something you commonly do. Unfortunately, when this happens you are directing your life with your thoughts, which are based on your beliefs. Your beliefs are based on your experiences and perceptions; so, while true for you, they are not always accurate. When you direct your life through your thoughts, it is not possible to be who you truly are and live life through your heart or true self.

Thoughts

Living life without thoughts, what we refer to as thoughtlessness, allows you to be in a state of neutrality, free of judgment with awareness.

You have the ability to be in any experience without attaching to it and to remain conscious and aware. Here you still feel but you do not attach meaning to those feelings and you can respond consciously and deliberately.

<u>Thoughtlessness in its highest form is pure awareness.</u>

<u>Live life through your heart</u>

Adele: Most of you may not understand the words, "living life through your heart." I thought that I clearly understood this concept at the beginning of the process. 'Yes,' I would say, 'I feel! I live life through my heart. I feel love from others and I love people.'

Understand that I was loving people from my mind. I would say the right things -- very loving things. I was a master at it. I knew how to care for people and take care of their needs. I also was good at giving presents – very heartfelt presents, ones that touched people's heart.

I wasn't truly loving from a feeling place. I know this because today, when I love, it feels entirely different. It's called unconditional love.

In the past, I avoided feeling deep inside or being truly intimate with someone. I had been hurt in that feeling place once before. <u>Why would anyone ever want to go there?</u>

I loved people from a mental/emotional place – through my patterns.

<u>No worries if you still don't understand,</u>
<u>you will start to feel differently as you go through this process</u>

Michael: Okie Dokie! Now let's discuss your <u>thoughts</u> for a moment.

Pooling Your Thoughts

Thoughts are based on beliefs and belief systems.

Remember, beliefs are assumed truths. Whatever you assume to be true about the world and your reality is based on what pool of thoughts you access your thoughts from.

Thoughts are actually measurable with today's science. Every thought and combination of thoughts has a particular frequency based upon their intent and the person's individual consciousness.

Thoughts that are alike have similar frequencies. They begin as separate things and then join together and form what we will call energy pools. These could be pools of greed, drama, despair, happiness, trauma, abuse, depression, anger, pride, fear and many more.

In order for you to think a thought that belongs to a certain pool, you must have beliefs that have a similar frequency.

We refer to these pools as Energetic Fields of Influence (EFI). These EFIs impact all of us and you will attract others from the same pool leading to life altering experiences.

<u>For a deeper understanding of EFIs we have a entire course on</u>
<u>understanding Energetic Fields of Influence (EFI).</u>

Michael: *EFI's are levels of beliefs that are associated with the typical emotions, guilt, grief, pride, shame, fear, anger. These EFI's are where all your human qualities start to develop that are associated with your belief systems.*

Human emotions are always associated with a belief system. Without the belief system the human emotion will not exist.

Beliefs are what give you access to the energy fields/pools. Your beliefs allow you to access that type of thought and/or give you the key to a particular pool of thoughts. The more you think the thoughts, the more you strengthen and/or support the belief; and the more you remain attached to that energetic field.

You won't have certain types of thoughts unless you have a belief that connects you to that energy field because thoughts are what lie in those energy fields. If you are connected to a particular energy field, then these will be the types of thoughts that will enter your mind or be accessible to you. Theoretically, you could fall into a pool of thoughts and drown in them, simply meaning you could get lost in thought or think obsessively. You are not limited to one field/pool but typically you have a primary one and access to multiple others. For instance, someone who feels shame has access to the pool of shameful thoughts and behaviors and if they think these thoughts too much, they may get lost there and live a life of shame.

Adele: Above is a very brief and simple explanation of beliefs and thoughts. There is much more to learn about beliefs and thoughts that can help you understand them better.

In the interest of time, we cannot include all of that information in this guide but for a deeper understanding, go to www.adeleandmichael.com.

<u>Not now! We recommend AFTER you complete this guide for that deeper understanding.</u>

Michael: Do you know that each and every thought and belief is an energetic pattern that can and will be explained and understood as quantum physics gets more advanced? <u>This is basically quantum physics in the human experience</u>.

Adele: Oh, no! Are we talking Quantum Physics now?! Please define quantum physics briefly and as simply as possible.

Michael: Sure! Quantum Physics is a bit abstract but it is the fundamental rules of the universe. People would be shocked at the Quantum Physics Theories behind many of the things that we have in our everyday life, let alone, to function here.

The only thing that you have to know is that there is a science behind this entire process that involves people's belief systems, patterning and core programs.

I know, this next part will be a bit of a stretch for the average person but as we speak, science is beginning to prove this. I have waited 30 years for the mathematics of Quantum Physics to prove it!

Adele: Hey, Michael, I wonder who you were in a past life. Physicist, Hermann Minkowski, possibly?

Michael: Real funny, Adele.

<u>But It Is True! It is Real for ME!</u>

If your thoughts continue long enough, they become your beliefs and you assume they are true.

In this state of consciousness, everything you experience seems real to you but in reality, it is only your beliefs that make these experiences real. They feel real to you because you believe in them.

We, as human beings, tend to look outside ourselves to make these experiences real and validate you and your beliefs, but nothing outside of you can ever give you the answer or fill the void within you.

<u>The void you feel withincan only be filled with your own connection to you or Source.</u>

Adele: That's for sure! For me, my beliefs about my body and my feelings of being dirty, gross and wrong as a child were very real to me. There WAS a void within but certainly not filled with my own love and connection to source, only distorted patterns and perceived beliefs.

Michael: This process is practical and based on unconditional acceptance and love with a deep understanding of the human experience and condition.

Taking Ownership

Once you accept a belief as yours, you see the world distorted and created by those beliefs

For instance, if a child is told he/she is bad, worthless, doesn't matter, she/she will most likely begin to accept this as truth, as his/her own belief. Changing your beliefs, changes your reality and what you see or experience.

You are not your beliefs; you are the creator of them!

Exercise J

Now take a few moments and write down things that cause you difficulty and begin to see if there is a theme in your thoughts, like sadness, disappointment, pride, shame etc.

1. _____

_____

_____

2. _____

_____

_____

3. _____

_____

_____

Becoming a Conscious Observer

Becoming a conscious observer is looking at your beliefs without judgement from a neutral position.

When you become a conscious observer, it gives you the ability to detach from your beliefs and decide which beliefs serve you and which ones do not. Then you can pick and choose what actions or behaviors you want to use in any experience.

Your behaviors aren't bad or wrong. It's just that up until this point, they have been based on your beliefs and that you have been reacting to life unconsciously, based on beliefs you were unaware of.

In other words, you are not a slave to your beliefs when you are a conscious observer. You can choose how you want to think, feel and behave without the influence of what you have been taught.

Once you change your beliefs, you can stop having this autopilot response to your experiences and your behaviors can be tools that you can pick and choose, like tools in a toolbox.

<u>It's that simple.</u>
<u>Change your beliefs, you will then change your behaviors automatically</u>
<u>and thereby change your experiences.</u>

You are not a victim of circumstance nor do experiences or things just come toward you because you believe things. It is more that you resonate with experiences that match what you believe in your conscious or unconscious. It gives a whole new meaning to the phrase 'birds of a feather flock together' doesn't it? Think about it, if you have certain ideas and beliefs, you will consciously or unconsciously draw to you experiences that match or experiences that you will interpret as matching.

So, if you are tired of having a particular experience or are encountering the same type of people in your life, you may have to look at changing your beliefs; therefore, changing your experiences.

Adele: For instance, I had kept attracting the same type of victimizers in my life, until I changed the belief.

Finding THE Truth

There cannot be a thought without a belief system to support it.

Once you create a belief and believe it to be your truth (belief), it attaches to you and becomes yours.

People never question these types of 'truths' because they assume they are true even if they are false. So, a little exercise that you can do in your life is to begin to discover these hidden truths or beliefs.

<u>Question Everything…. especially that which you do not typically question!</u>

Adele: I questioned everything. I questioned every manipulating thought, every creepy feeling from others, and every self-abusing thought/feeling about myself.

By doing this, I began to discover the things that I have always just assumed or taken for granted, as truth.

Hopefully upon investigation, you will find that many of these things are not true.

Did you ever notice that when people become defensive, it is when their beliefs are being challenged?

Why do you think this is?

Why do people get defensive?

People get defensive because their beliefs are the foundation on which their ego and identity are based and if their beliefs are wrong then they are wrong or often feel wrong.

Adele: For instance, all my life I thought that I was a team player. My identity was an athlete that knew the meaning of teamwork. I would get along and was agreeable to almost anything. I would give myself away or subtly manipulate to get what I wanted.

But as I got deeper into this process, I realized that wasn't the case.

When someone would question me, I believed that I had two choices. Either submit to them or push them away, defend, fight or make sure that I had the upper hand.

What we have found is that most people do these two things:

1. Some do it sweetly and know how to subtly attempt to manipulate others to get what they want or shift the experience to their liking.

2. Some are not so subtle; they push, fight and argue.

Both scenarios are not balanced.

A balanced experience would be for both parties to listen to one another and together, as a team, come up with a solution that best fits the situation. Note: Sometimes making a compromise is not an option. Sometimes, you just have to make the choice to choose something different for the benefit of the team.

<u>Why do we allow our identity and ego to get in the way of a pleasant, smooth, collaborative team experience?</u>

Because you believe you are our identities and beliefs, you believe what you think is true and accurate when it comes to our emotions.

Michael: I will use a husband who was raised by a screaming mother and a wife raised by a quiet father.

Example I

Mary is angry with Frank because he forgot to pay the heating bill. Mary begins to yell at Frank "how could you forget? You know we have two small children and it is the dead of winter!" Frank stands staring at Mary and in a split second, he sees his mother berating him and thinks "I wish she would shut the hell up! I didn't do it on purpose and yeah duh I know it's freakin winter. What do I look like? A dumbass?" Why don't you just ask me what happened?" Mary looks at Frank just staring at him and in a split of second, thinks "He looks just like my dad. No response, no emotion, no answers. I have to do everything. Men are just a waste and never help you."

Now you can see they both have beliefs and judgments about the opposite gender and are presuming they "know why" the other person is doing what they are doing. Little does Mary know that Frank had to rush his best friend at work to the hospital because he had a heart attack and came straight home for some consoling. While Frank has no idea that Mary is so overwhelmed by the children's behavior that she is at her wits end.

Here we see two sets of beliefs blaming, judging and responding without any communication and each party reacting to the other internally. This happens every day to most people. They both believe their internal talk as truth, which creates great problems and long-term resentment from nothing. If you don't resolve this way of being, you will end up isolating yourself in business, family and partnerships and possibly ending these relationships.

Adele and I decided to resolve anything that had an energetic charge in our lives or anything big or small that would stress us out! We decided that if we were going to be on this earth, we might as well enjoy every interaction emotionally, physically and spiritually.

This is what you should know about teamwork:
- Together, as a team, choose the right idea that benefits the whole team.
- Unified focus toward a common experience or outcome.
- . Being an integral part of something while maintaining your individuality

About the Ego

The ego is basically a belief system, a set of beliefs of a person that tells the person who they think they are or who they are supposed to be.

Going back to the fighting ego aspect... You do such things because you are typically not conscious and the ego and belief system run your life.

The ego is based on a created identity and this identity is based on beliefs.

While we are part of 'Source' or 'God', while you are here on Earth having your experiences. Your egos, are separate from Source in order to be here and experience.

The ego is the one who carries that belief of separateness, so that you can function on the planet and interact with others. The problem is the ego is like a small child that wants what it wants and will do whatever it takes to get it.

You simply have to retrain it, so You can work with it rather than let it control you. The ego operates using your behavior patterns that are based on your beliefs and belief systems. When beliefs are challenged, the ego, its structure and the identity are threatened and it must protect itself.

This protection often appears as defensiveness, disbelief, doubt, argument, hostility, withdrawal and demanding proof to total denial or avoidance. What usually happens when someone is called stupid or ugly? Typically, they either verbally or physically attack the other person by calling them names or they withdraw and runaway.

Why? Because the ego and self-esteem have been told that they are not good enough or valuable and their identity must save face and salvage some worth, so they attack or retreat to avoid exposure of their flaws.

Keep in mind the truth never defends itself nor does it try to convince or convert.

All of your experiences and beliefs support the behavior patterns used by the ego which is an attempt by the ego to maintain its belief system and identity. The beliefs for each person may look different but they all have the same goal – maintain the current belief system.

Self esteem is the ego's opinion of itself!

How Beliefs Run the Show

The beliefs sometimes fool you by getting you to think the belief is "over there" or about something or someone other than you.

By falling for this misperception, you do not realize it is in you! Therefore, you do not notice it is running your life while it keeps you in its loop. When you are in a pattern, meaning you are charged or feeling an emotion, many times you will not know you are in a pattern. It's like you are in a loop and unconsciously responding to situations and people around you.

When you judge your beliefs, you are admitting they are real and that you have to "do" something to deal with or combat them. Nothing could be farther from the truth. Judging your beliefs creates an emotional and mental attachment to them. Once you create this attachment these beliefs have become yours!

Exercise K

Write down a couple of things that you currently believe about your neighbors, coworkers, family members, your spouse or partner.

1. _____

   _____

2. _____

   _____

An Explanation of how Belief Systems are Formed

Beliefs eventually turn into belief systems.

A belief system is a complex design of multiple beliefs creating an entire system.

This belief system could be completely self-created or adapted from a family belief system, a cultural belief system or all three.

Examples of Belief Systems:

1. A family belief system could be "If you want something done, you have to do it yourself," or "if you show your vulnerability in the family, you will be attacked."

2. A cultural belief would be something like, "Women are inferior," or "Only the strong survive."

3. It could be men work and support the household and women stay home and raise the children.

Within each person's belief system, there are often unique variations to the cultural or family belief system. Belief systems are like opinions: everyone has one and everyone has slightly different ones.

However, just because you have a belief system, does not necessarily mean it is accurate or that it serves you well. This is why you should question everything and then discern and decide if it is working for you.

At some level, life itself is actually a belief system. Because of this you can actually create any type of life you wish.

Becoming aware of your beliefs and belief systems frees you from their limitations and allows you to create a different experience.

Take out the list that you wrote about what you believed about people and remember this:

- What were facts and what weren't. Unless you have fact, Remember whatever you just had written about these people were simply your perceptions or judgments.

- If you do not have facts then it is completely a story.

- We make judgments all the time about who people are, what they do and why they do things.

Freedom from Beliefs

By having this freedom, you may then recreate a new conscious perspective on how you wish to understand, see, feel and experience life.

This then creates a new vibratory frequency in your energy field. By changing your beliefs, you change your frequency or vibrations. It then allows you to become a creator rather than a victim to your beliefs and belief systems.

Remember, your beliefs will support your intent. You may intend to ignore the truth and create a fantasy reality, or you can see things as they truly are.

By seeing and interpreting life clearly, you can actually create the life that you want by changing what you believe rather than be governed by a belief system you are unconscious of.

- Some will say this is nonsense

- Some will say - wow this is freeing

- Others will be too fearful to do anything.

Which one are you?

What do you believe?

People will hold onto their beliefs as long as they see a payoff or benefit to keeping them. They will fight to the death if they believe those beliefs serve them at some level. Usually there is a subconscious belief that is being served when it is difficult or impossible to change a belief.

People often say, at this point, how can that possibly be? How can I possibly be using a belief that doesn't seem to work for me and yet it still serves a purpose so I am unwittingly holding onto it.

Example of Benefiting from a Belief

Let's say you are the type of person that constantly makes verbal mistakes or is unclear in their conversation to the point that people make fun of you or you appear to be unintelligent.
You might wonder how someone could continue to do this behavior and how there would be anything that would be of benefit for them to continue this type of behavior.

I will give you a very quick answer as to why.

Someone who does this could have a belief system that tells them that they are stupid or unworthy. Any of these beliefs could cause someone to unconsciously create the behaviors; we just gave you an example that fulfills and sustains the lack of self-worth that the individual has for themselves.

In other words, if I believe that I am stupid and unworthy, I will unconsciously <u>set myself up</u> and place myself in situations that make me look stupid and unworthy. This will confirm my belief about being stupid and unworthy.

This is a very small and brief example, but every human being has beliefs and belief systems that are supported by behaviors that at times make no sense at all.

<u>Again, consciousness cures everything!</u>

There is no pill for being conscious. There is only you becoming aware.

Adele: If you are not conscious and aware of your behaviors that come from your beliefs, you will always stay stuck and pertaining to the above example, you will continue to appear and feel stupid and unworthy. You will create circumstances that create the outcomes of what you believe you are.

<u>Basically, something from your past is telling you how to live in the present.</u>

Once you recognize and see that your fear and the experience is no longer possible today because of the awareness that you have developed, you will no longer live in the past.

<u>You will then be free to release the belief
and see the experience as benign,
freeing you from the pain or suffering.</u>

As long as you carry what you call pain from the experience and choose to hold onto it, you will maintain that belief. When you want to hold on to a belief, you will find yourself fighting to the death and finding every excuse why it is true or justifying your feelings in order to keep it.

The major problem with beliefs is that you are not consciously aware of them and tend to believe things will happen based upon your past experiences. This puts you in the position of understanding and experiencing present events based on your past; therefore, you are never fully in the present.

It is like having a filter over your vision as you look at your experiences. This prevents you from experiencing the "now" because you are experiencing the now through the past.

<u>You can never be fully present or experience something truly new if you are perceiving life through
your beliefs from the past.</u>

<u>Your past beliefs limit your present experience</u>

Remember what we said earlier, about living and loving people from your mind. If you are in the past or future, I guarantee, you are in your mind.

Living in your heart, and using your mind <u>only</u>
to navigate around the earth, means you are in the present

*"The Mind is just a translator of what you feel in order to
communicate and understand living on earth."*
Michael Cavallaro

Adele: True!

Michael: Once a belief is etched in stone…

Adele: Wait, stop, my dear! Let's say we take a break, instead.

You may want to go get another cup of coffee or tea or water and meet us back here in 10! Ready...break!

I am serious! Go! :)

Okay welcome back!

Michael: Okay, can I continue, Adele?!

Adele: Oh Yes, please do.

Keeping the Belief Alive

Michael: Once a belief is etched in stone, accepted as truth, your ego goes to work to support it by creating experiences that support and defend that belief. The ego must also support and defend it.

If confronted by another's belief, the ego will try to discredit their challenges and prove its own beliefs. The deeper the belief, the harder and more threatening it is for the ego to let go of it. The removal of one belief now threatens other beliefs. Because of this, many beliefs are going to protect themselves and the defenses will become stronger and more intense the closer you get to core beliefs.

For instance, if you believe that, 'other people judge you,' No matter what anybody says, you will find negativity in their statement to prove that they are judging you. This is the ego working overtime to hold onto and justify that belief. The ego has many tricks up its sleeve to support and maintain your belief systems. This is where it gets tricky.

Trickery at its best! Sometimes your pattern will fight. Just remember your consciousness, your essence, is the part of you that is running the show!

Because you are in the energy or frequency of being judged, you will also be critical of others and judge them. This will keep you in the energy of being judged and will trap you in an endless cycle that you can't get out of. You will keep yourself trapped and won't even know you are doing it. Sometimes it seems like it's almost impossible to change.

It is possible.

Exercise L

Write down some beliefs that you have about yourself.

_____

_____

_____

_____

Going Deeper

What we have experienced and know to be true is this:

In order to change beliefs completely, you must clear their energetic charge from the mind, brain, neural pathways and emotions. The energy of the belief creates its own neural pathways, so that every time you have an experience in that energy field, it will use and access those same neural pathways, making them even stronger.

Our belief systems are part of our being.

Changes MUST take place in a person's belief system, thought processes, their brains (energetically), their brains' patterning, their mental and emotional aspects and their hearts and souls for change to be permanent.

It can get very complicated if you are not careful, so I am going to give you a few tools to keep it simple.

- No matter how sure you are, question everything! Especially those things you've never questioned! By questioning, you can find the source and discover if it is factual or nonfactual.

- Pay attention to evidence. Don't skip past something because you think you have already figured it out. A good rule of thumb is that if you think you have something figured out or believe you know it all, you probably don't.

- Look at your beliefs carefully and fully evaluate them before you make a decision about them.

- If you are afraid to question a belief, it's a good bet that there's a falsehood or lie in your belief system or that you are hiding something.

- Your job is to question with curiosity, inquisitiveness and the openness of a child – pure in nature. The absolute truth will always withstand any amount of observation and questioning.

Make Some Changes

While you are working on your beliefs, change your behaviors because if you stay in the old behaviors it supports the beliefs and makes them harder to change.

Your behaviors are like food for your belief system so by changing your behaviors, you are basically starving it into a place where it has to change to survive.

An alcoholic is a great example of this. If the alcoholic is your belief system and the alcohol is your behavior, once you quit using alcohol, you will go through detox, in other words, you will change your beliefs. While this can be very uncomfortable, once you have detoxed and changed the beliefs, you no longer need the alcohol, aka behaviors, because you have shifted your belief system. The only time you will pick up a 'drink', so to speak, is if you go back to the old belief systems.

The Answer Isn't All in Your Mind

To become a creator of your experiences, you have to be conscious and aware of your thoughts and your beliefs.

This process is about working with the mind yet expanding your knowing to understand that Quantum Field is where the charges that drive the mind reside, even if there is no associated belief or memory.

This is why precognitive traumas (traumas that occur before a child has words) are more difficult to resolve through counseling or therapy.

<u>Clearing or restoring the frequency patterns to their natural state is what completes the transformation of a person.</u>

<u>This is why working with the mind is never enough.</u>

Adele: This was a tough one for me. There was a point when I understood my experience of sexual abuse so clearly. The important word here is…<u>understood</u>. I understood these experiences through my mind. I never felt the experience. I stayed in my mind.

No matter how much I understood the experience, the feeling of my wound was still present. The reason why I know this is because when I would get triggered from a current day experience that would remind me of my past, I became charged. An emotional charged memory would surface and I would try to bury it quickly and attempt to jump back in my mind. Or I would numb myself with food, busyness, alcohol or whatever.

<u>You will always have memories.</u>

<u>The *charged* memories are what disrupts your life.</u>

An example of a charged memory would be what affected a person, pre-cognitively or cognitively; the feeling of a memory – the hurt, shame, fear, embarrassment, etc.

Adele: For years, I attempted to convince myself that the charged feelings/memories were no longer a part of me.

<u>Just because you understand something, doesn't mean you are over it.</u>

I had a strong desire to be completely free of this pain of the charged memories. It reached a point where my mind could not convince me any longer that I had resolved the pain of the abuse. I still felt the charge.

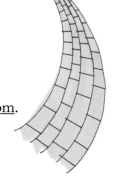

<u>My mind is not what controls me!</u>

<u>Consciousness is the answer!</u>

<u>Consciousness and self-awareness are the keys to your freedom.</u>

Exercise M

Please answer the seven questions in the blocks provided.

CLEAR YOUR HEAD

7. What are the thoughts that you are fearful about?

1. What memories do you get stuck on, that you can't seem to get past?

6. What thoughts do you have about others?

2. What are some ruminating thoughts that you just want to go away?

4. What thoughts make you angry?

3. What words trigger you into an emotion?

5. What thoughts bring you joy?

Helene Huber

Adele: You must get in touch with the things that are swirling around in your mind. Then you must <u>feel to heal</u>, those things, in order to have the freedom that we speak of.

<u>Can't say this enough!</u>

You just have to touch on these self-abusing, ruminating, controlling patterns to be able to break them loose and unravel your ball of yarn that I mentioned at the beginning of the chapter.

Michael: And I can't <u>say THIS enough</u>!

Courage brings the conscious transparency to the soul and allows the human to align. This means that when you have the courage to face yourself, your beliefs and patterns you then make accessible your connection to your own soul which then allows for your human and soul to connect and live from your inner wisdom. But this often takes the courage of the ego /personality to allow your consciousness to become aware of your belief systems and patterns.

Adele: Beautifully said! I Love you.

Michael: I love you, too! But save that love talk for the Tin Woodsmen's chapter, Adele!

Adele: Chapter Five is The **<u>LOVE</u>** Chapter!

Chapter Four
SUMMARY

- Your identity and judgments

- You are more than just your thoughts.

- Creating everything that you experience or bring to yourself means that some conscious, semi-conscious or unconscious aspect of you is bringing an experience into your conscious awareness, so that you can resolve or change any belief or core program that is not love.
- Most people think that bringing it to yourself comes from you being aware of what you were creating -- this is false. In most cases, it is an unconscious aspect of you creating the situation.

- Core programs create core patterns which create beliefs. Beliefs create thoughts and thoughts spur behaviors, all of which are supported by perceptions and judgments by the ego/personality of the individual identity.

- Beliefs become assumed truths which make up a belief system.

- A belief system is a complex system of thousands of beliefs assumed to be one identity. A beliefs system continues to sustain a core pattern by feeding it with perceptions, experiences and behaviors to prove it to be true.

- Those core patterns feed the core programs. It is what we will label as a feed-feeder system. All of these systems feed or feed from each other to keep it alive.

- It forms a frequency grid to allow the beliefs to manifest in a person, consciously and/or unconsciously, which then allows them access to the Energetic Fields of Influence (EFI), which then manifest with physical and emotional display.

- When the individual can stop the feeding, by becoming more conscious, the old dysfunctional belief system begins to fall apart, and they begin to see and experience the world differently.

- It's not just the abuse that creates the belief system, it is the belief system of the family and the family patterning that gives foundation to the beliefs and perceptions or possibility of the abuse.

The abuse does however create common beliefs and perceptions for everyone despite the type of abuse.

• Beliefs and perceptions are key to transforming the wounds of abuse as they allow access to the feelings which are <u>the key</u> to complete transformation. Feeling here should not be confused with emotions as emotions are based on beliefs and perceptions. Emotions are not true sensate feelings.

> **Beliefs** = mind and mental
> **Perceptions** = mental and emotional interpretations
> **Emotions** = responses to beliefs with charges felt in the body
> **Feeling** = the ability to sense the quantum field without the mind (sometimes called intuition)
> **Patterns** = ordered energetic quantum field designs
> **Programs** = the codes that create quantum field patterning

• Your Ego

• **Concepts #7** *Everyone is ready in their own time.*

• **Concepts #8** *Feel to Heal*

• <u>**Exercise J:**</u> Things that cause you difficulty and seeing if there is a theme in your thoughts, like sadness, disappointment, pride, shame.

• <u>**Exercise K**</u>: Things that you believe about your neighbors, coworkers, family members, your spouse or partner.

• <u>**Exercise L:**</u> Identify some beliefs that you have about yourself.

• <u>**Exercise M**</u>: Scarecrow Design

<u>Okay, are you, now ready to learn about that middle area of your body?</u>

Ya know the place, where your heart resides.
The place where you sense feelings that may have been confusing at times or the awareness that makes your heart pound because you are surprised, scared or in love.

Or the feeling of butterflies in the stomach or the tensing up of your intestines that cause you to become irregular. Ha!

Adele: Okay! Are you ready…for some
Open-Heart Therapy?

Turn the page!

Chapter Five

Loosening up the Heart

Tim (Mann)

So why would we even need to loosen up the Heart?

Why was it closed in the first place?!

Adele: I am certain that a newborn who opens its eyes for the first time and looks at its mother, doesn't say, "I don't trust you. I will close my heart now."

No, it looks at its mom, as something that is a part of them – something that it has been attached to for nine months. I don't know the sensate energetic feeling when a baby feels it's first physical touch nor when the umbilical cord is being severed after it exits a mother's protective womb (Fortunately or unfortunately I do not remember).

Although I would imagine that the infant feels something, as it is touched, and then cut, by the doctor/midwife for the first time.

Twenty-seven years ago, I remember thinking, which doctor do I want to have the honor of touching my daughter for the first time? The doctor that I chose was very knowledgeable and logical, yet I could still feel his kind heart in there when I looked beyond his stuff, what we call, programs and patterning today.

I would imagine that an infant would sense all these feelings but certainly not judge what it was feeling, rather it would stay open and just experience and observe what was happening.

At what point, do we as humans, close our hearts?

<u>When we begin to judge, instead of observe or just experience!</u> **That's when!**

Michael: When we make meaning to other people's behavior and then perceive the world based on those perceptions, we are living in a distorted reality that never leads to an open heart.

The Heart of a Child

The key to every human being is their heart - **Michael Cavallaro**

- *When you connect with the heart of a child, a child knows that you love them even without words.*
- *A child's heart is open and innocent when it comes into the world.*

If you care for a child's heart and teach them to love <u>themselves first,</u> you open a world of unending joyful possibilities to them. Raised in this way, a child knows that they are loved, even if it is unspoken.

Loving a child does not mean allowing them to do whatever they want or not being firm when necessary.

Loving a child means teaching them to be functional in life while loving themselves

<u>You are the guardian of a child and their heart.</u>

You are their guide in life.

Preparing them for life and loving them is the greatest gift you have to offer. A guardian, parent, foster parent, an older sibling or cousin or neighbor, aunt or uncle are a child's guide in life. Their job is to prepare a child for life and loving them unconditionally is part of that preparation.

Here's the problem in the world today; when you abuse a child in anyway, you are part of the reason that a child closes their heart.

When you abuse a child because you are playing out a pattern or a belief that you were taught, you dull a child's sparkle.

Adele: Sometimes it's tough to admit when you have dulled a child's sparkle.

I remember an experience re: dulling an individual's sparkle, like it was yesterday. I can still picture my two daughters' innocent eyes staring back at me.

My oldest daughter was about four and my youngest daughter was about one and a half.

Example I

Dulling Someone's Sparkle

My ex and I had a fight. He then left the house; Then my oldest asked me a question. I ignored the question and started yelling about our Labrador's hair being all over her clothes. I went on and on! As I yelled, I suddenly became unaware of my daughter's presence and only aware of my anger. In fact, I didn't even visually see my child, only my ex's face, and he had left the house!

I continued to rant and rave. After I was finished, my daughter's face reappeared and I became more aware. My daughter stood there staring at me. It was first time that I actually watched her energetically shrink; her sparkle that was present just moments before, had dulled. Literally.

<u>I watched her sparkle disappear right before my very eyes!</u>

I was crushed and felt tremendous guilt. This girl had sparkle most of the time. Fortunately, I had the opportunity to stay home with her for about the first six years of her life and we literally played together most of the day, creating and learning things, exploring, dancing and playing ball. I had been a teacher for three years prior to giving birth to her, so I just continued to teach.

So, back to the sparkle. I not only saw her sparkle fade, but I then looked at my youngest and she too was staring at me. Sparkle still intact, but she stared with the most confusing look on her face, like she had never experienced her mom's anger coming out of a loud voice.

Obviously, our fight had nothing to do with the children, but because they were present in those circumstances, it had everything to do with them. I should say, <u>everything to do with affecting them!</u> They didn't know that our fight had nothing to do with them! Nope, they only felt the angry energy in front of them.

<u>And that is where it begins, folks!</u>

It was highly probable that my daughters both made up stories in their minds about what that experience meant to them. I wasn't skilled enough at the time to explain to them that I had taken my anger for their father and threw up all over them. (Not literally, but certainly energetically.)

Their dad and I rarely fought but when we did, we almost always had our disagreements behind closed doors or managed to compromise on things in front of them.

So, this experience was new to my daughters, not new to the concept of hidden anger, because they both witnessed plenty of suppressed anger in their few years of life. They finally witnessed the angry energy "out in the open" with words to go with it.

That was the day that I started searching for answers to these feelings that were inside of me. I could not bear to see those faces react like that again.

I was not aware then of the patterns and beliefs that were being modeled for my daughters, I was only aware that I felt something not good that day, something that dulled their happiness.

As they grew, I watched how certain things affected them.

I started working on myself and going through this process when my two daughters were around 8 and 6 years old. I discovered so much through trial and error. I worked this process in my own style but used the basic tools that I had been given by Michael.

I used each of the tools only when I was ready for them. There were different stages for different tools. I only used the tools that worked best for my situation.

I taught my daughters in a way that they would understand, as I learned. Because of this process, my daughters have benefited greatly and their direction in life was forever changed.

Keep in mind, I have shared with you the subtle things that we do as humans that damage a child's sparkle, not the obvious abuses, such as physical and sexual abuses.

Although what I observed that day when I yelled at my daughters was in fact, verbal abuse. I have found that this process works for any type of abuse.

Michael: Abuse is anything that…IS NOT LOVE!

Exercise N

Go to a time in your life when you felt good, light, at ease, safe and loved. Recall a situation where someone's words or actions caused you to feel that feeling, or sparkle, dull. When did you feel the need to close your heart? Look for where this feeling reoccurred.

1. _____

_____

2. _____

_____

3. _____

_____

4. _____

_____

Exercise O

Recall three situations where you noticed that your actions or words dulled the sparkle of someone else:

1. _____

_____

2. _____

_____

3. _____

_____

Having your sparkle dulled or dulling someone else's sparkle, are things that are not easily forgotten. Some people can hide what was done for a while, but I guarantee you that when you get triggered, they will return.

Example II

Who knows what will happen when memories are triggered.

I once pulled a chair out from someone who was just ready to sit down and she fell straight down on our third-grade classroom floor, which resulted in many students to laugh at her. I wasn't friends with her and I didn't really know her well. I thought it was funny when I first did it and enjoyed the smiles once again as class clown, but just for a moment. Seeing her face and imaging what she felt like, as she sat on the floor, as the other kids in the class continued to laugh at her, not so much. I felt so bad about what I had done.

I always felt guilty and it never really went away. Here's how I know.

When I was in my forties, we met again. I saw her at a mall, went up to her and the first thing that I said was "I so apologize for pulling the chair…blah, blah blah." Instead of saying, "Hi! How have you been since grade school?" Nope. That was the first thing that came out of my mouth. I probably sounded like an idiot.

I was so lost in my memories of the grade school incident that just seeing her face again triggered the memory. I was unaware of how I looked as well as blinded by my guilt. That is what we call not living in the present because my past was not resolved. <u>My past was triggered. Well this guide is about using your Inner voice to assist in finding those triggers, so that you may LIVE in the Present.</u>

Well, fortunately, this woman was very nice about it and said, "Oh Adele, that was such a long time ago, but thank you." Then we laughed about it.

Perceiving Things Through the Senses

All humans are living satellite dishes

Michael:. Human bodies are living satellite dishes receiving energetic/vibrational feelings from the environment 24/7.

Adele: They really are!

Michael: They live their lives receiving through the sensate feelings, meaning they perceive things through the senses.

Adele: They really do!

Michael: Really? Adele? May I continue.

Adele: Ha! Just kidding.

They live their lives through the sensate experience —all of life is sensed through the human body at all levels, conscious or unconscious. These senses are not to be confused with emotions. Senses and emotions are completely different!

Emotions are the interpretation of the senses based upon the belief system; therefore, for all human beings, environmental experiences affect them in some way, shape or form, consciously or unconsciously.

The sensate experience could be things like a sound, an action, a movement, a person, a place or thing, a temperature, a smell, a visual, a vibration, a frequency, etc.

Adele: So, for instance, in the example re: my daughters, the sensate experience for my daughters could have been the sound of my voice, the movement of my spinning around the room while I was ranting and raving, maybe the smell from the kitchen of something baking while the experience was happening or simply the visual of their mom's angry face.

Michael: Exactly! So when a person grows up, a sensate experience/memory can be triggered at any time.

Adele: Pleasurable or non-pleasurable! A pleasurable sensate experience could be a holiday, the smell of cookies, the visual of lights or maybe family members surrounding you. So, you will chase after that feeling, maybe look forward to a holiday to feel good or bad.

Why do you think there is so much depression and disappointment after a holiday? Maybe because you had to gather all this perceived pleasure into a couple of days and then go back to a perceived non-pleasurable life. That seems kind of ridiculous, don't ya think?

Now a non-pleasurable experience during a holiday could be the opposite effect. Maybe there was so much abuse and uncomfortable things during the holidays that it triggered an unpleasant experience.

Do ya get really what we are saying?

These pleasurable and non-pleasurable experiences that we mentioned may trigger your
- Core programs
- Patterning
- Belief systems
- Behaviors

When a sensate experience awakens one of the above, those systems turn on automatically and the person may experience whatever is triggered, such as:

A happy, sad, anxious, stressful memory
A time that they heard a particular song
An experience in a sport activity – maybe an amazing acknowledgment or an embarrassment
A smell, touch or sound
Something traumatic – physical, emotional, sexual, spiritual event

Example:

A Sensate Experience

As my oldest daughter grew up, I would frequently notice that when I raised my voice, I would feel her react internally and there was nothing I could do about her reaction. Most likely she believed that when I raised my voice, I was probably angry at her because she did something wrong.

When I was upset or angry internally, she would always ask me, "What's wrong, mommy?"
Even though I knew that I was limited to what she would hear from me, when it came to her growth, I would always tell my daughter that she wasn't responsible for my feelings, as I would watch her attend to my feelings most of her life.

The only thing that I could do was try to explain it to her, but after a while she was tired of hearing it. You see, I couldn't truly help because I wasn't the one who perceived the trauma, she was. They were her own triggers that she formed as a small child; therefore, she at some point, will need to trail back to find those memories.

Then one day when she was in her twenties, I decided to explain to her about her family patterning and why she did some of the things that she did. She was open to it because she had been taught some of this process since the age of eight.

I said to her, "Listen, girl, if we are going to have an close adult relationship, you have to speak up and tell me how you feel. You have the right to say what you are feeling and what you want out of this relationship. You are only responsible for your own feelings"

<u>Everything changed after that day</u>

The relationship is continuously evolving of course, but it seemed that something inside her woke up that day .

My younger daughter had a whole other set of beliefs about how she perceived her childhood experiences. Don't assume that children from the same family unit will have the same perceptions and beliefs.

<u>Each human interprets differently from their own perspective.</u>

<u>You cannot assume anything.</u>

Michael: Next are but a few questions to answer to begin to understand and discover what your beliefs, thoughts, judgments and feelings are. Beginning with these and looking back into your life will really benefit you.

Exercise P

Answer these questions:

What types of things were said to you and/or about you during your childhood that you still believe today?

_____

_____

_____

How was conflict handled in your family?

_____

_____

_____

How were you spoken to as a child?

_____

_____

What feelings or events influenced others to change how you were spoken to?

_____

_____

How did your parents talk to each other?

_____

_____

How did your parents behave towards you, each other and other people? How were those behaviors different?

_____

_____

Look at your answers and you will begin to see how you have been unconsciously programmed to behave the way others believed you should or you thought you should based upon what you witnessed.

This has formed your identity and who you believe you are. In most cases, 80 - 90% of what you believe about yourself does not even belong to you. This is why the things you believe about yourself have come about because of others and your interpretations of what others have done or said to or about you.

<u>Now add to this what beliefs or perceptions of yourself were created
as a result of the abuse you experienced.</u>

This is not to invalidate what you feel but to understand why you feel what you feel. Things in your life have been distorted and corrupted by other people's belief systems and your own misperceptions and misunderstandings. This does not change the fact that they are real to you. We completely understand that the feelings that you feel are very real to you.

What we are sharing with you is that even though they are real to you, they are created by intentional and unintentional programming from your environment and the misperceptions that we all create ourselves due to our lack of understanding of how the world works.

Exercise Q

Read the words in each of the boxes on the suit of armor and focus on the feeling that they inspire in you. List words to describe the feeling that you associate with those words. ex. anger: hatred, hot, unjust, rage, yelling, unsafe. Once complete, answer the questions.

Are you guilty or ashamed? Explain. Be specific.

_____

_____

Why and when do you get angry?

_____

_____

Are you spiteful? Explain.

_____

_____

Are you manipulative? Explain.

_____

_____

REMOVE YOUR ARMOR

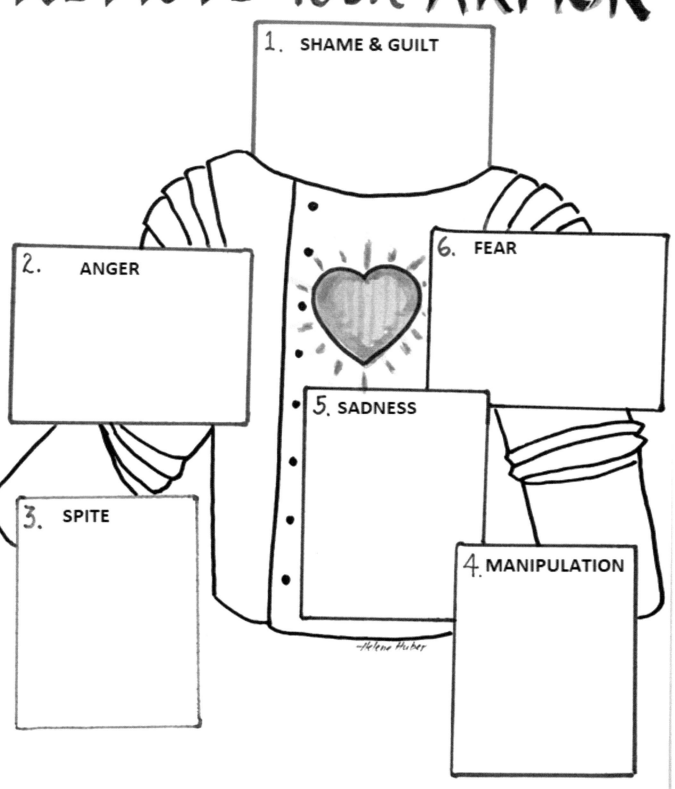

1. SHAME & GUILT

2. ANGER

3. SPITE

4. MANIPULATION

5. SADNESS

6. FEAR

Are you lonely, sad about your past relationships? Explain.

_____

_____

What feelings are you afraid of?

_____

_____

Where do you feed off or create drama in your life?

_____

_____

What is your definition of love?

_____

_____

Why do most people avoid feeling?

Self-honesty

Michael: Self-Honesty is difficult when it comes to trauma. Because of your trauma, you have most likely learned to keep secrets and not be honest with your feelings. You may have been told not to tell; therefore, honesty with yourself may be more difficult.

<u>Self –honesty requires the end of denial!</u>

Self-honesty too, is required for permanent transformation. This does not mean telling others about your discoveries or inner life, although that may be included by your own choice. This does, however, mean that you are in conscious awareness and self-reflection while admitting to yourself all of your discoveries. In other words, there is no denial.

When you decide to be honest, it's important that you learn to not judge yourself and your discoveries. For self-judgment is the source of much of your pain.

Some people are honest about the pain, but admit the pain with the intention of punishing themselves and suffering as if it were a penance for what happened to them. But this is not necessary. Self-judgment and self-punishment only serve to enhance the wounds and never serve the transformation of your wounded self.

Self-honesty with non-judgment allows you to integrate your self-discoveries into a new and reawakened state of being where you will begin to live and regain your lost joy and happiness.

Self-reflection, self-discovery and self-honesty create the doorway to transformation.

As long as you keep secrets from yourself, you will not be free from limitations.

Concept #9

*Keep no secrets; secrets separate and destroy – **Michael Cavallaro***

Secrets are a big part of abuse: whether you were told not to talk about it or you were too ashamed to talk about it yourself.

Keeping a secret is a denial and a form of hiding from yourself.

Keep no secrets from those you love, your spouse, your children, friends and/or especially yourself. Each secret, no matter how small, unimportant or large, is an invisible wall you place between yourself and others.

Michael: Both of us as children saw things that others were trying to keep quiet. We both spoke of those things when others told us to be quiet. This is what got us in trouble, becoming known as the loud mouths and trouble makers.

Secrets destroy intimate relationships with others.

Adele and I didn't want our relationship to be destroyed or separate us; therefore, we disclose all of our secrets to each other. As the years rolled by, we consciously committed to sharing those secrets as they arose. Yes, some secrets were difficult to admit and some came before others, but we were patient with each other and understood that each of us was ready in our own time to reveal them.

Secrets at their core are kept to deceive or to avoid rejection and perceived pain. They truly serve no positive purpose in an intimate relationship. There is no such thing as a good secret. People often justify keeping secrets by saying they will hurt someone. You can only hurt others if that is your intent or if they interpret what you said as hurtful. Sometimes your secret is that you want to humiliate others or put them down in some way, but not appear to be doing it. Sometimes your secrets are hidden in sarcasm. Sometimes your secrets are to avoid judgment, and so it goes.

Examples I

Keeping secrets to yourself, so you don't have to admit what is really happened.

Adele: One of the secrets that I kept about the groomer/counselor was the fact that he hurt my heart. I also didn't want anyone to know that <u>I felt so embarrassed, ashamed and stupid for being duped.</u>

Duped: A person who is easily fooled or deceived.
Unwittingly serves another person

Examples II

Another secret that I kept to myself for a long time was that I was embarrassed to admit that a family member had influenced me to perform oral sex on him. <u>I felt ashamed and stupid for participating</u>, even though I was only six years old.

I chose to keep these secrets, holding on to my hurt rather than admitting this hurt and possibly calling them out. I didn't want to look stupid or helpless because a part of me believed that it was my fault because I had participated in this act. I know now that it was not my fault and I did not deserve to experience this abuse. But holding on to this secret was exhausting.

My failure to speak up may have caused him to repeat the same pattern with another. There were other victims before me and others after me. This was tough to look at the fact that I didn't speak up and I knew that it was happening to other girls just like me. I really didn't see the big scope of this situation until I was in my forties.

These experiences had affected me and each one of my future relationships. I lived life keeping these secrets hidden, waiting for my partner to turn on me and cause me pain, which created conflict within myself, as well as in each of my relationships.

<u>This is what we call not living free from limitations.</u>

What are the secrets that you still hold true about yourself. Something that is hidden/tucked away or something that is right there on the surface.

<u>And then after you write those secrets,</u>
<u>Go buy a safe to keep them hidden from others.</u>
Just Kidding…

<u>Well maybe not!</u>

Attempt to bring your secrets to the surface in some form, so nothing about you is denied or is a secret to you. An example would be, I felt so embarrassed, ashamed and stupid for being duped or I felt ashamed and stupid for participating.

Exercise R

- _____

- _____

- _____

- _____

Most people have difficulty doing this.

If you are remembering something about your past, there is no need to LIVE there, or dwell on it. You are simply visiting that place of pain and all your perceptions of how it made you feel. Again, you are just visiting. You are observing for your own self-discovery. This type of writing most likely will bring up some fear, hurt, shame, etc. Remember, at this point in the guide, you are just visiting these experiences, there is no need to dwell on them.

Confessions to Self

When you confess things to yourself without judgment, it can be very freeing. We are not talking about the day-to-day trivial confessions that you make to yourself, we are talking about simply owning your participation in your life experiences, traumatic or otherwise.

Your human tendency will be to hurt and blame those who have caused you pain, but no matter what occurred you were still there willingly or not.

Adele: For instance, when the priest/counselor approached me as a 14-year old, (refer to my story) he had given the appearance of a healthy fatherly love that I longed for.

As a small child, I believed that love meant giving myself away. This misperception of love worked to the priest/counselor's advantage. It played right into their hands. These root beliefs set me up to be taken advantage of. But where do these root beliefs come from and why did I choose to believe them?

<u>Being honest is the admission of truth and fact.</u>

While it would have been easier to blame them, this would have kept me a victim for the rest of my life and perpetuated the cycle of pain. In order to free myself from the never-ending cycle of pain from this experience,

I had to confess the fact that I placed myself in that position. Was I a naïve innocent young girl who had already been sexually abused? Yes. Did I deserved to be duped by older men? No.

But the fact remains that I did place myself in these positions

Admitting you were consciously or unconsciously an *Unwitting Participant,* means you were SIMPLY present during the ABUSE that took place.

Before you throw this guide up against the wall, please hear us loud and clear. We fully understand that you have been traumatized by your abuse.

An *Unwitting Participant,* means
you were **SIMPLY PRESENT**
during the ABUSE that took place.

Being Present

During my sexual abuse experience, was I or was I not present for this experience? I was present. Were they individuals who took advantage of my wants and needs? Yes!

I participated in these behaviors and let them into my world. Again, am I condoning their behavior? NO, I most certainly am not. They were wrong on so many levels. I am simply owning my behaviors. And what I wanted was answers to LOVE that I had lost as a small child.

<u>We hope you want to keep reading.</u>
<u>Addressing this topic is very delicate and challenging for most people.</u>

We acknowledge your pain and suffering and whatever was done to you. NOBODY deserves abuse in any form.

It is almost beyond most people's comprehension to see themselves as an unwitting participant. We care about each and every one of you, so, trust me when we say, try to keep an open heart and mind. You will soon begin to understand this - trust the process.

If you are stuck here and can't move on and this guide is already on the floor after hitting the wall, (that was a joke) perhaps you are not ready yet. Maybe you need a little assistance, a one-on-one, with one of our trained group facilitators or one of our recommended therapists. (More information on this is available in the back of this guide.)

<u>Just don't give up. Hey, you came this far!</u>

<u>We are here to tell you that the pain you feel doesn't have to continue and there is HOPE!</u>
<u>Oh, you are Back! Wonderful!</u>

<u>You created the experience; therefore you can undo it!</u>

<u>You created the experience as an unwitting participant.</u>

Let me say it again.

You created the experience as an <u>unwitting</u> participant.

Because you have created the experience, the opportunity now, with this new information, is to understand what you perceive about the experience. We will get to this!

<u>Back to that question again.</u>

<u>Why would a person close their heart?</u>

Adele: Before this process, I believed that I had an open heart. I was a kind person. I enjoyed most people. I always tried to see the good in people, although I did judge the not-so-great side of people, of course, quietly in my mind.

Today I understand that as long as I am judging others, my heart is not fully open.

When I judge another, I am only judging them because I judge myself.

Redefining the Open Heart

Michael: Typically people think that an open heart means that you feel emotional and that the heart opens outwardly toward others. And I would say to you, "An open heart from a higher perspective has nothing to do with emotions."

<u>An open heart from the higher perspective means that your human is directly connected to your soul and spirit; thereby integrating and living your human life with a fully, connected, divine experience that is yours from your god-self.</u>

<u>An open heart opens inward toward self and your soul!</u>

Commonly, the human experience has been relating to others and finding others to stimulate your heart center or emotional connections. It is also meant that by "connecting with another," you would feel somehow fulfilled and whole. This is a type of feeding or emotional vampirism.

So, know that an open heart does not need another for a relationship; but it may have relationships with others from a whole perspective rather than, "I need something from someone" perspective.

If you notice closely when you need something from someone, you'll notice you are feeding. When you need to be like others, or do what the "norm" is, you are again in the feed/feeder cycle. This is not wholeness and this is not an open heart.

The feed/feeder cycle is when someone gets fulfillment or emotional nourishment from another person, place or thing. This is what the old vampire movies were based on and they used blood as the metaphor for food.

An open heart, with the connection to your spirit, lives each moment as a full experience without fear, without hesitation, without doubt, without need. It is full living or should we say, "living life to its fullest;" and, most of all, without needing or wanting another person.

This is the hardest thing to understand because your whole life as a human being, you are typically told that you need someone else to be whole; to look for a relationship, to find a mate, to find someone to fulfill you or your needs. Now combine that with what you see in the movies; what you have seen or heard as a child about how it feels to be in love or to have your heart open. We will tell that this is level one limited consciousness that never allows for a full experience of living with your heart open and only creates the illusion of it.

Adele: Again, try to see the possibility of what Michael is saying. This will help you later in the other chapters. If you don't trust me because you don't know me, just call or text me or maybe we should email back and forth to get to know one another. Anyway, continue, Michael!

Michael: Thanks, Love!
I am only setting the stage and do not expect for you to fully get this concept that I am presenting. So please don't run away and if you are having trouble just let this part go for now.

And Adele I am glad that you changed that last part to emailing/texting, otherwise I would never see you!

All too typically, it is taught in many of the new teachings or writings that you might see in the public, that an open heart is the way to go. And yes, it is. But sometimes, people don't explain what an open heart means. It is often left to people's own assumptions from their past experiences and what they have either read or heard to determine what living with an open heart means. So, let's revisit living with an open heart at its purest form.

Living with an open heart is being connected to self; and to know that until you are connected to your own inner self, and we use the word "inner self" at this time because often it is said "higher self." And we would say to you that "higher self" is a misrepresentation for exactly what is going on.

You are you at all levels. So, there is no "higher self;" there is no other self; there is only self. And so, we are referring at this time to "inner self" just to have clarity.

Let's compare the "inner" versus "outer" self. There is the inner self that is your spirit, your soul, all of the knowing from your oneness and your god-self. The outer self, what we are referring to here, is your human self; your human identity that relates to the external world as some form of reality.

The only reality is your reality. And all too often you believe that because you are experiencing something that other people can relate to, that it is somehow universal reality. This is not true. And it is a difficult concept to grasp. Your reality is yours and yours alone. No one lives the reality or perceives the reality or feels the reality exactly the same as you do. There are those that feel something similar; and because this is describable and seems relatable, people mistakenly assume that it is the same reality.

You have come into this world to have an experience of some sort. And in order to do that, there are overlapping commonalities in everyone's reality so you can either see, feel, touch or come in contact with others.

In order to have those experiences, you have to have some overlapping, common realities. Living with an open heart, at its purest sense, is the same for everyone. Your heart is open and your divinity, your spirit/soul, whatever you would like to call it, lives through the human experience - creating its own experience.

Your heart, located at the physical heart center, is at the gateway of this connection. It is non-physical, although it resides in the physical. And having that gateway open is living with an open heart. This truly is what living with an open heart means. And when you live with an open heart, your soul/spirit integrates into your human experience and becomes one with your human existence.

If you learn not to relate to your identity with your birth name and the individual that you have believed to this point that you are, you recognize that you are so much more and so much greater than that limited perception; and the "all" parts of you meet and experience the human existence from a greater experience than you could have from that previously limited identity.

Once the heart, or the gateway to your spirit, is opened from your human identity, your spirit and soul walk into your life; and there is no longer a higher self, a middle self, a lower self. There is only You, capital Y o u.

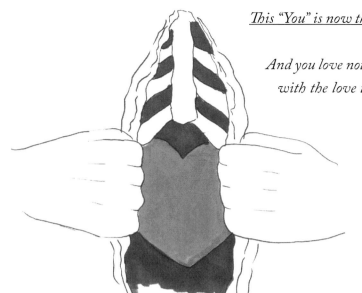

This "You" is now the living embodiment of a loving heart.

And you love not because you love others; but because you are filled with the love that exists in those aspects that you were not connected to within yourself because that is what you are - pure love.

Pure love, at our soul/spirit level, does not need to love others; does not want to love others; does not have human emotions as you may have known love to be up until now - **Michael Cavallaro**

Adele: I love that! You know, Michael, you should write a book with a bunch of little sayings in it, your know,, just a bunch of inspirational quotes.

Michael: I have a book like that, Dear! Remember, the amazing Nancy, put it together. It's called, *Ramblings!*

Adele: I know, Sweetie! Just messing with you.

During this transition and conscious change, it is sometimes quite awkward living from a pure heart rather than living from a human identity that loves from the limited perspectives you were taught or came to believe. This loving is because it is your essence and your nature. You do not treat people differently. You tend to judge less and less as you begin to integrate. And the love that you feel for your existence is what love is.

And because you feel the love of your Essence, your divine nature, other people feel that and interpret it through their human identities and perceive you as loving. But they do not realize that when you are in that state, you are merely reflecting to them the love that lies within their own "heart gate" that they too could access if they searched to live with an open heart from this higher perspective.

All too often humans project the lack of their own inner connection onto others to seek a reflection of a miniscule amount of the love that lies within their own heart gate. And when they find someone who loves more than they love themselves, they then perceive that person as being extremely loving and honor that quality. But what they do not realize is that they are actually honoring themselves.

<u>For somewhere they know that it too lies within them</u>
<u>and that they are the love themselves.</u>

This HEART chapter that is smack dab in the middle of this guide! It is the purpose of the guide!

You are searching to find your Inner Voice and then Transforming yourself from the Inside Out to feel and Be Love! But what else do we need to get to this love!

It is a bit challenging to find the love within your own heart and not need or want anyone else; to know that you are solely fulfilled and sovereign within yourself because it means letting go of the ego/personality, the identities that you have assumed to be yours, that you have been watching or taught since birth.

Letting go of those identities and those ego structures is terrifying to the ego/personality. And the ego tends to hold on and seeks to project a mirror reflection of its own love onto others so that it can experience a form of that love without actually having to give up the ego/personality's identity and programs. At times it seems very scary, even terrifying, even confusing.

<u>But that is all an illusion once you get past a certain point.</u>

You will find that all of the things that you were afraid of - afraid of letting go; afraid of not needing others; afraid of being alone- all disappear without effort when you open the heart gate and live with an open heart.
Remember that an open heart means that your heart opens inward to your disconnected parts of self, which in this case is your soul/spirit. It does not open outward to others.

It is a curious and very different thing than anyone has ever taught or instructed.

<u>But in knowing this, you should find it easier to know that the door to your</u>
<u>heart that you have been trying to open outward actually opens inward.</u>

Imagine trying to open a door in the opposite direction against the hinges--it would be impossible for it to open completely . And yes, you should know, it does feel like your heart is opening; and we assume that it is opening outward to the world. But in truth your heart is opening inward to a larger and greater world than you have known to this time.

<u>So, look to your inner self.</u>

<u>Go through the gateway of your heart and go inward.</u>

Even the ancient mystics spoke of going inward. This is what they meant. Focus your consciousness inward and the heart shall open. As the heart opens, your inner truth reveals itself to your human consciousness.

<u>When you open the gateway, the heart inward, you move toward becoming your own source.</u>

And know that until you become your own source, your own sovereign being that is integrated with your divine aspects then you can live and love with an open heart.

The metaphor for loving yourself is also something else we would like to address here. Loving yourself does not relate to anything that you, to this point, have defined as love. Loving yourself is taking the focus of your consciousness; placing that focus on your inner gateway of the heart and your heart opening; reconnecting with your soul/spirit, your divine self, whatever metaphors you would like to use. And once you have reconnected, then you are in love (in the love) with yourself meaning that you are and have become the love that you truly are. This is what loving yourself means.

Adele: Okay, Marvel, STOP! No really, that's enough! He still cracks me up today when he goes off or should I say UP to, I don't know where the hell he goes, to retrieve information like this.

Michael: Okay Dottie! And let's make something clear. I am right here retrieving the information here on earth, like you. It's time now to bring the universe and heaven here on earth, instead of waiting until we cross over, remember?

Adele: And then he says things like this that makes so much sense. And yes, I do remember, Sweetie!

Self-Love

You have to call yourself on the game to stop the game even though everyone is playing the game. That is self-love.

Your expression of self-love is your way to freedom. When you become a living example of self-love, your children will be free from their cycle with you and allow them to find their own living example of self-love. When you love self, you free everyone connected with you and you become free. This is why it is only always about you, never anyone else.

You must love yourself more than you love anyone; and then, a funny thing happens. You then love everyone. Until you give up the idea and the attitude that you have to love someone else, you are distracted and cannot completely and one hundred percent love yourself; and when you one hundred percent love yourself then there is love for everyone. You cannot love anyone more than you love yourself.

You can only have your heart broken if you love someone more than you love yourself - **Michael Cavallaro**

Love Yourself

Loving yourself begins with accepting yourself as you are.

This means physically, mentally and spiritually. What you think of yourself is only a judgment based on perceptions you accepted as truth as a child. How many of you have thought how hard it is to be here? Loving yourself allows you to interface and play here with joy._

What exactly does loving yourself mean?

Well let's define it as this:

Unconditionally accepting who and what you perceive you are. Your body is a gift Mother Earth has given you on loan. She has loaned you your skin and bones.

Adele: I love that!

Michael: When you judge your body, you judge the earth because your body is borrowed and made from the earth. It doesn't matter what your body looks like, it only matters that you love it.

Take care of whatever shape you have. It's a vehicle, take good care of it. When you dislike it, and don't take good care of it, it starts to break down. When you judge it you are saying it isn't good enough. Remember the shape of your body is about your issues.

When you love yourself you automatically love the earth.

<u>When you hate yourself you automatically hate the earth</u>

<u>When you accept your body, you accept the earth.</u>

<u>Your body is just a loaner from Mother Earth – appreciate it.</u>

Your spirit is the real you, not your thoughts or beliefs of who or how you think you should be. Please stop judging yourself. This alone will bring you happiness and peace. How you experience your journey is your choice!

Loving yourself - this is a funny statement used a lot and few people seem to really understand what this means. It begins with accepting yourself as you are without judgment physically, mentally, emotionally and spiritually. Loving yourself allows you to play on earth happily. The love spoken of is the love of the Christ Consciousness, the love Jesus spoke of. It is not human love. It is not romantic, sexual, sensual or family of origin oriented.

<u>It is Divine love brought through you in its purity of an open heart desiring nothing</u>

<u>and sensing the oneness, beauty and wonder of all life.</u>

This love means putting aside your desires, needs, attachments and most of all, your mind.

<u>This love is pure and exists because it exists and seeks nothing in return.</u>

You are not your body but you live in it, so take good care of it so it will last long and be enjoyable to be in. Not because there is a "health craze" and not because everyone tells you to be healthy, but because you would like a nice comfortable ride while in it. If it is miserable to be in your body, then you feel miserable, so make the body feel good so you feel good in it.

The next and very important reason to love your body is that you will automatically love the earth. The earth has loaned you a piece of herself that makes your flesh and bones. So, if you love your body you love the piece of earth you are borrowing and thereby love the earth. This will help her to make her changes more smoothly and you then get to experience her changes with joy not pain. Earth changes can be avoided by being conscious. This then changes your consciousness and hers and she doesn't have to have a trauma to change nor do you!

Human consciousness has the power to create or destroy. Negative attitudes and thoughts destroy. Positive attitudes and thoughts create! (Real positive attitudes come from your mind not your head, false ones come from your mind with thoughts or trying these are not effective in change only looking like change.) Are you for real? Do you really love?

For those of you who are losing your sense of reality, control and ego, my apologies, I promised Michael that he could be free to talk about all aspects of the heart and as long as he wanted.

Love Chemistry

Love is that calm, peaceful, gentle, pleasant feeling, not high, not low.

All of those emotional rushes and feelings in your body that you got when you thought you were in love and associated that with love is not what love is.

You just feel good where you are, wherever you are; and there isn't a high and there isn't an emotional rush. It is not that kind of love.

This is why we talk about that definition of love. Using the word love doesn't really work anymore because the meaning has been so distorted. And people try to associate that with the love that they had when they were growing up and the excitement and the feeling and all that. And then they never quite feel that love anymore and they get confused while they are chasing it.

Human love relies on chemistry. Real love has no chemical rushes. It is just the state of beingness that from a dense, tense or stressful state seems like bliss.

Love of Others

You cannot truly love others until you love yourself.

Until then, you will only have glimpses of what love is, and in most cases, any displays of love are simply external, intended love so that it is perceived as being loving. It is not the true essence of love in most cases; but, because it is perceived as loving or loving gestures, people define this as love. Love itself just exists and there is no need for display.

When you unconditionally love yourself, you will find that people feel or sense love simply by being in your presence. There is no need to love them. Because you are love itself, people will experience love. But they will not experience it because of you.

> You will be the love in the outside world that will remind them that they are love and
> they will remember and thereby project the definition of love onto you
> because they do not yet have it within themselves.

Adele: I mentioned this earlier about Michael modeling love. This was what I was referring to. When does a drop of water realize it is water? Or is it just water and never has a realization because it is the existence of water? This is the same with love. But human beings chase love as if it is something that they can gain. They say they love others because this is what *they* want and they were told to do. This is a great dis-service for the world at large because it keeps you chasing something outside of yourself.

Could you imagine if the entire world said "do not love anyone else and spend your entire existence loving yourself"? Where would the businesses be? Where would the banks be? Where would any economy be if everyone on the world simply spent their focus on loving and pleasing themselves and not in a narcissistic way, but in the pure essence of love being the experience of love itself?

> Remember that you cannot love others any more than you love yourself.

So, when you find yourself wanting to love someone else, it is probably a message to yourself that you need to be loving to yourself. And from now on, please use the phrase "unconditionally accepting of self" as a replacement or interchangeable with the word "love". In doing so, you may find it easier to unconditionally accept your ego personality displayed behaviors and you will then be able to move toward finding your essence.

Too many people spend their entire lives blaming and trying to work out the issues of the ego personality while they miss the essence of themselves. While a smaller minority spends too much time trying to love themselves and ignores the ego personality. Doing one or the other is an imbalance; both must be used, learned and mastered.

So, in mastery of self, you must unconditionally accept your ego personality, you must master the appropriate behaviors to manage life on Earth In doing so, you must also open up and understand, accept and feel your inner self which is love itself and is unconditionally accepting of everything that you do. It is only the lower self that causes you to make judgments of yourself and others and how others should love, love you, or you should love or be loved by them.

Adele: Alright Marvel, bring it back to earth.

Michael: I am on earth, Dottie! Remember, I just brought Heaven TO Earth!

Love, Intimacy and Sex

Love, intimacy and sex are three separate things often confused as one.

Lets define these things:

Love - pure, beyond human emotion, divine love and self love, love of/with another or for another.

Intimacy- closeness

Sex: The physical act of sex

Adele: Love, Intimacy and sex. I am so grateful to have been able to sort out, understand and experience these three words in this lifetime, the way every human being deserves.

After many years of wanting to be normal in these three areas, it became abundantly clear that most people are NOT normal and are dysfunctional when it comes to these three words. I would imagine it's because of our family belief systems as well as our cultural beliefs.

Today, I know that love means loving myself and all aspects of me purely. It's as simple as that. All aspects of me includes everything from my toes to my skin, hair, and nose. Being intimately sexual with a partner requires for me to love every part of me from my head to my toes, to my issues and my nose. It also means loving my emotions, sensate feelings and my pure essence.

Being physically intimate (Otherwise known as making love with another) is loving yourself so deeply that you can share yourself with someone else.

Michael: I want to comment on the words, *making love* which is often associated with sex and another person. Now I am going to be a bit of a stickler here, so be prepared.

First, I believe that you cannot make love, you share love! You may share of yourself and/or your body. Second, sharing love does not mean you have sex, but you are intimate. Third being intimate does not mean you have sex or share love. Fourth, sharing love may include all three.

- Having sex equals using someone to have an orgasm. Being sexual with someone may be using someone or sharing love.
- Being intimate is being close with or without love.
- Sharing love maybe sexual or non sexual.

It is all in the intent of the individual.

Would it be nice to say I shared myself with so and so and it was beautiful rather than I had sex with? Aren't you truly sharing your heart, yourself, your love and your body? Sharing implies conscious choice and equal participation.

Keeping Secrets to yourself

Adele: Keeping secrets to myself was one of my biggest dislikes. It tore me up inside. Keep a secret, and I guarantee you that there will not be any chance for self-love. Self love requires transparency.

Keeping no secrets in my life was very big for me; admitting the things about myself that I hated or despised. Those judgments came from my patterns, something that I gave meaning to, and/or something that was perceived by me whether it was true or not.

I realized that I couldn't be free from self-judgment until I forgave myself on all levels for everything I judged about myself. Forgiving myself for behaviors that I chose in my past allowed me to love myself again.

This self-love led me to the intimacy with others, and the Love that I knew was possible.
Things became really clear when I began to shed some of these judgments about myself. As they faded, I began to feel the love that was inside of me, that was hidden. This happened gradually, over time.

If you think that the phrase, "love that was inside of me" is too corny and stupid, how about, I began to feel comfortable in my own skin, felt a sense of contentment, ease, fulfillment and calmness that I had only briefly experienced before.

Again this change was gradual and subtle. But internally, it was brilliant and life altering.

<u>You begin to see what real kindness to yourself looks like.</u>

Concept #10

Be Kind in All Things - **Michael Cavallaro**

Be kind to yourself first! Be kind to others. Be kind in all your deeds and the way you speak. If you don't feel kind, at least act kind. Eventually, your insides will match your outsides, as long as you are willing to do what it takes to change the root of your unkindness. But acting is not enough; it's just a beginning.

If you plant the seeds of kindness, then you will eventually harvest kindness. Often, when you start to plant kindness, you expect an immediate return. However, you must remember that the seeds you planted earlier must complete their cycle and that harvest will eventually come. Your intent needs to be pure. It's not about what you get in return.

It's about kindness—for its own sake and the pure intent that comes from your heart. You will not always be successful, so be especially patient and kind to yourself as you learn that it's not about being perfect, it's about being kind.

Sometimes kindness for the greater good appears unkind to those unwilling to change. You must discern your true intent when you take action and not worry about others' perceptions or judgments; only you will know if your intent is truly kind.

Adele: You come first. You don't put yourself down or give yourself away. It can be as simple as not giving yourself away during a conversation. In other words, stand there and say what you mean, communicate effectively, and don't give in to what others want you to be for them. Stand there and be present in your life!

Concept #11

Be present - **Michael Cavallaro**
You must be present in the moment to be fully in the body and to experience life to its fullest, to experience the moment. You must also be mentally, emotionally, physically and spiritually in the now to live fully. Being in the present allows you to have memories. If one is not present, then who is there to remember? At that point, only the unconscious is present. The unconscious records everything; the conscious mind only remembers when it was

there. The conscious may access the unconscious, but it is often a long process. In the present, there is no depression, no anxiety.

Depression is being in the past: it's your perceived tragedies or losses of the past that are interfering with your life today. Anxiety is being in the future: it's the fear of perceived danger, pain or the unknown.

Have you ever done something you found so engrossing that you lost track of time, and thought of nothing else? This was being present. When you are truly in the present, there is no fear, no sorrow and no time; there is only the experience. However, being in the present does not eliminate issues, even if they appear to be gone.

Being kind and being present is an amazing gift to give to yourself. Doing things for yourself is wonderful, but if you do things for others to get something from them, that is a whole other thing.

Here's where it gets a little tricky.

Owning Your Stuff

Owning why you are really doing something.

Adele: When I became aware of how much I did things for people to get something in return, I was shocked. Catering to other people's emotions, wants and needs was a common occurrence for me. Most people didn't even notice this happening, for God sake, I wasn't completely aware of it myself.

Of course, that was not the case with my partner. Michael noticed everything! He brought everything to my attention! This began on day one of our relationship. As we started to apply this process everyday, things started to change! Wait, no, let me correct myself. It was every second of every day that we applied this process. We lived AND worked together.

Even though we applied the process, there were still things that I didn't want to let go of.
Everyone is ready in their own time, right?

I loved this concept during the times that I wasn't ready to let go of things so I could still run my patterns, try to deceive, blame, make up stories, and miscommunicate because that worked for my ego and patterns.

When I wasn't willing to change something, I did the, "You are not accepting me, Michael, for who I am," statement. "This is just how I am. You should love me for who I am!"

Michael was very patient with me. Sometimes, I pushed him over the edge when I would informed him about the things that I was doing for him out of kindness, although I knew deep down that I had an ulterior motive. He once said to me, "Do you realize, Love, that you are attempting to run the same patterns as you did with your ex?" Aaaaa! That statement was difficult to swallow. It's difficult to hear something that you don't want to admit.

Michael: He would also say "I can love you for who you really are and not like what you are being like or not like your behaviors, right now!" LOL

Adele: Ha! Most things didn't bother him. He was very kind. The times that his buttons/patterns <u>were</u> pushed, he of course, would use the process for his own issues that came up.

I realize now, that I was in fact, abusing Michael. I beat him up, had him in head locks, flipped him in the air where he would fall hard on the ground and couldn't get up.

Michael: That was painful and I cried a lot when she did that to me. I lost any sense of manhood! How embarrassing.....LOL. Could you imagine, Adele, the fairy that she is, flipping ME in the air?

Adele: We are joking, of course, about flipping him in the air, although, I did in fact abuse him regarding my dysfunctional ways - like crying to get attention, being spiteful, disregarding him, making up stories about how I thought he was behaving and poking at him relentlessly.
There were so many ways that I kept the patterns going. I continued this dysfunctional lifestyle until each and every one of these patterns no longer served me.

I have to admit, seeing Michael's face, after each and every time I abused him, was not pleasant.

When you love someone so much and you believe that you cannot stop your patterns and emotions from running the show, it is not a fun place to be in.

Is your partner putting up with your dysfunction of abuse?

<u>Only you know!</u>

And trust me, <u>you know</u>!

If you are still abusing another and you are not ready to stop, you don't have to judge it, but at least admit it.

Remember:

Seven Steps to Freedom (1)

Knowing that you are unhappy where you are and desire to change

Seven Steps to Freedom (2):

Awareness of what makes you unhappy.

Adele: I started to become aware that this experience of verbally and emotionally abusing Michael was not making me happy. I didn't like the way I felt inside., while accusing him of being the source of my created pain.

So, why was I making my home an emotional litter box?

Concept #12

Don't make your home your emotional litter box - **Michael Cavallaro**

This one is huge, but almost all people ignore it at some point in their lives. A litter box is where a cat leaves its excrement. You often leave your emotional excrement at home and are nicer to strangers or people you do not live with. You carry around your stresses all day and then you go home and release them. For example, you may be short-tempered, impatient, grumpy or intolerant, and then wonder why home is so unpleasant.

If you come home and yell at your children, ignore your spouse or demand things in a rude way, is it any wonder that the feelings at home are combative, hostile or empty? Is it any wonder people at home would be less than welcoming? As a result, work, friends, school or anywhere else becomes the place you would rather be. Home becomes the dreaded place; other places become your haven. Home should be your haven.

Home should be a place where everyone feels safe. You are often kinder and more patient with strangers, acquaintances, co-workers and friends than with your children or spouse. Shouldn't your spouse or children be treated with special care? Always treat those you love with kindness and respect.

Below are a few more concepts that were mentioned earlier.

Concept #13

Own your behaviors – **Michael Cavallaro**

When you own, or take responsibility for your behaviors, you accept that you made them and therefore can change them. When you blame others, you deny ownership and assume the position of a victim. Blame is stating that something outside of you controls you. This leaves you feeling and believing you are powerless, and so you are. Your behaviors are always your choice. Even if it is an unconscious choice resulting from your internal programs, it still comes from you. Remember, your behaviors are always your choice at some level, whether you are conscious of it or not.

Concept #14

Eat Crow to Grow – **Michael Cavallaro**

Simply put, you must look at your issues and own them in order to grow. As a result, you may have to eat crow, which can be hard to swallow. But if you can admit and own your flaws, poor attitudes, imperfections and judgments, self-abuse then you can truly grow. It is your feelings of not being good enough that drive you to be perfect. As a result, you often avoid looking at your imperfections because it can lead to disappointment. Then, when you finally have to admit that you are not perfect, you feel so much pain that you wish to avoid it at all costs.

In the end, your unfulfilled expectations, lack of unconditional self-acceptance and your inability to admit your flaws, mistakes, creations or errors are what caused you discomfort. Denying them you remain frozen in the past, in a life of self-deception, denial and you cannot grow.

If however you admit your flaws, poor attitudes, mistakes, judgements, errors and creations, you open yourself to a world of opportunity. You'll find yourself in the driver's seat with the chance to make different choices and do things differently. But the only way to get to that place is to admit these things. It's your choice: will you eat crow to grow?

Adele: You have made it to the third Step to freedom! Yay you!

Michael: Yay!

Adele: Michael, are you making fun?

Michael: No, just joining you in the enthusiasm. I love watching you when you get passionate about things.

Adele: Well, Okay, then!

This is the **third step** to Freedom!

Seven Steps to Freedom (3)

Accept responsibility for your behaviors and choices

Now that you have become conscious and aware of the situations in your life and have the desire to change, it is time to start taking responsibility for your behaviors and choices. This can be very hard for most people because they're operating on autopilot and have never taken the reins on becoming truly conscious about their life.

Responsibility doesn't mean that things are your fault; it just simply means that you are the creator of your life whether you made decisions consciously or unconsciously you are the creator. Most people see life as though it is happening to them and they are simply navigating the stream.

<u>You are the oar directing your canoe, you are not the canoe!</u>

You are the creator of your life and that life doesn't happen to you; you create it. If you can accept that this is a possibility (or even a reality) you are well on your way to having a life that you want.

You are not a victim of life, other people, circumstances, or the universe.

<u>You are no longer a victim</u>

<u>You were a victim in the past</u>

<u>Now you are a creator</u>

<u>Owning your part</u>

(Don't expect anyone else to own their part. Remember, everyone is ready in their own time!)

Adele: I learned this process quicker than others only because I am a wonder woman or just maybe because I am an amazing human being who has mastered the human. Well maybe just the Wonder Woman part.

No, the reason why I learned this process so quickly was because there wasn't any wiggle room to slip back into my original patterns – not when you are living with someone like Michael.

What was I thinking?!

I WAS thinking. Michael was the best thing that ever happened to me; Best decision that I ever made!

For the past fifteen years, Michael and I have been working at these patterns. You can say it was an intensive personal two-person study. Did I try to hide some things? Yes! Was I sometimes very creative in hiding those things, yes, absolutely! !

Did I sometimes get angry because I couldn't hide things? Most definitely yes!

But eventually, it took too much effort to hide the secrets, it really wasn't worth it. This is where I had to get really honest with myself and sometimes had to admit that I was self-abusing myself very subtly.

Many times, I simply couldn't see what I was doing. These are what we call, blind spots.

I truly am so grateful for where I am now!

Each one of the things that I resisted in our relationship resulted in a payoff, a payoff to benefit me!

Because both Michael and I were in previous marriages and remembered the litter boxes that we created there, it didn't take us long to see and be aware of what we were doing in our current marriage.

There was also the desire to be free from this drama and pain and have a smooth partnership, so we could enjoy each other. It was pretty simple.

But I must admit, we were hard on each other, but we were committed.

Was it tough at times? Yes! Was it worth it, now? Absolutely yes!

Below is the **fourth step** to Freedom!

Seven Steps to Freedom (4)

Understanding the payoff or the perceived benefit of your behavior and choice.

Everything you do as a human being is done for a perceived reason or benefit. Even if what is occurring in your life does not make sense, it is still being done for a reason. Often times the illogical things humans do are being driven by a behavior pattern, a belief system or an emotional reason.

If there was not some reason or pattern behind what you did, you wouldn't do it.

You behaved a certain way for certain reasons or benefits.

Humans are simply driven by a behavior pattern or a belief system.

Freedom is the goal here. Right?

Freedom is when there is nothing outside of you affecting you, only love.

It's about loving yourself and understanding the self-expression of that love.

The most perfect transformation is the love of self, then the love of others and non-judgment of others.

In the next Chapter, you will have to ask yourself, do you have the Courage to do whatever it takes to move yourself towards love?

Or will you be driven by emotions, family patterning and behaviors of acting out - always the victim, always blaming, always in guilt.

Do you have the courage to face yourself?

It's so worth it!

Chapter Five
SUMMARY

- **<u>Seven Steps to Freedom (3)</u>** - Accept responsibility for your behaviors and choices

- **<u>Seven Steps to Freedom (4)</u>** - Understanding the payoff or the perceived benefit of your behavior and choice.

- **<u>Personal Identity:</u>** The collection of aspects, qualities or characteristics that defines who a person believes they are supposed to be; a person living up to the expectations they believe they are supposed to meet.

- **Concept #9** *Keep no secrets they separate and destroy*

- **Concept #10** *Be kind in all things*

- **Concept #11** *Be Present*

- **Concept #12** *Don't make your home an emotional litter box*

- **Concept #13** *Own your Behaviors*

- **Concept #14** *Eat crow to Grow*

- **<u>Exercise N:</u>** Things that dulled your sparkle as a child.

- **<u>Exercise O:</u>** Things that you have done that clearly dulled someone else's sparkle to fade as a result of your words or actions:

- **<u>Exercise P</u>**: What types of things were said to you as a child growing up? How did your parents talk to each other? How did your parents behave towards you, each other and other people? How were those behaviors different?

- **<u>Exercise Q</u>**: Tin Woodsmen design

- **<u>Exercise R</u>**: Bringing your secrets to the surface in some form, so nothing about you is denied or is a secret to you.

- If you care for a child's heart and teach them to love **themselves first**, you open a world of unending joyful possibilities to them. Raised in this way, a child knows that they are loved, even if it is unspoken. Loving a child does not mean allowing them to do whatever they want or not being firm when necessary. Loving a child means teaching them to be functional in life while loving themselves.

- You are the guardian of a child and their heart. You are their guide in life.

- Preparing them for life and loving them is the greatest gift you have to offer.

- Each human interprets differently from their own perspective. Admitting you were consciously or unconsciously an *Unwitting Participant*, means you were SIMPLY present during the ABUSE that took place.

- Your expression of self-love is your way to freedom.

- Love is pure and exists because it exists and seeks nothing in return.

- You cannot truly love others until you love yourself.

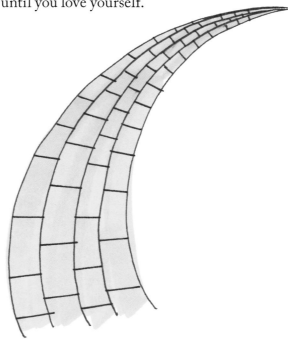

Chapter Six

The Courage to Change

Leo

(Courage)

Are you hiding from the world or not participating in life?

What is it about the world that prevents you from participating in it?

What fears do you have about fully engaging in the world?

How do those fears serve you and your beliefs?

Fear is a funny thing. At times, it may feel overwhelming or something that motivates you to move yourself out of a situation. Fear will arise at some point during this process. You may feel like you are going to or want to die.

Are you going to die? No, of course not; although it may feel like it and you may encounter a lot of fear.

There are often times during your transformation you feel like quitting; especially when there is sense of impending doom, great fear or a sense of death or an ending. When this occurs do not worry, it is normal during transformation to feel this way. This is absolutely the time to continue and push forward. This is when the ego and belief systems are on the brink of change and they may go into a panic and give you every message to stop your growth, that there is something wrong and it would be best to give up and run.

In its most extreme version this often feels like you are going to die. The truth is, there is a death coming. The death of your old self and the beginning of a new life! So, in a way, there is a death that will happen.

Think of it as D.A.I (pronounced die).

Download
Assimilate
Integrate

- What has happened during our time together is that you have been downloaded with new information that has begun to transform you.

- During the assimilation period is when the ego/personality realizes both consciously and unconsciously that the change is taking place and fears the elimination of an identity and makes an attempt to stop the transformation and hang on to the old.

- Once getting past this assimilation, the <u>integration</u> of the information takes place.

After this, everything calms down and the panic and fear usually dissipate for the time being.

<u>No Worries!</u>

Do your best to observe this if possible and do not buy into it. This will make your journey much simpler and easier.

Let's try something:

Exercise S

Please answer these questions in the blocks provided on the next page.

1. When do you freeze up and then give up something that you wanted or desired?

2. What words trigger you and make you want to quit or feel afraid?

3. Where in your life do you not Walk Your Talk?

4. How do you currently channel the energy of your wounded feelings? Do you get mad? Are you mean or bitchy to other people?

5. Do you think negative thoughts about yourself? Are you mean to yourself? Do you shut down?

6. What are some things that you would like to accomplish but every time you attempt them, something or someone stops it from happening?

Concept #15

You only chase what you believe that you do not have – **Michael Cavallaro**

You chase or try to acquire what you think you need or desire and believe you do not have. If you have something but don't believe you need it, you ignore it. On the other hand, if you don't think you need it and don't have it, then you don't try to acquire it. Just because you believe you believe you don't have something and chase it, doesn't mean that you don't have it. It simply means you do not see it.

For example, some people do not believe that they are loved, so they try to get it from other people and ignore the people who do love them. This is chasing love because they do not believe that they are loved. The fact is they are simply blind to the truth that they are already loved.

They were just not loved in the way they expected it to appear. This chase is a coping mechanism to fulfill unrealized needs or desires. This way of being can never permanently change your life. Whatever is acquired is always temporary.

Exercise T

What do you still desire but do not chase?

1. _____

_____

2. _____

_____

3 _____

_____

4. _____

_____

Exercise U

What do you desire and still chase?
Things that you believe that you do not have.

1. _____

_____

_____

2. _____

_____

_____

Adele: We have come up with six stages regarding abuse and recovery which is part of the entire Human Mastery process. This guide is just a piece, among the thousands, yes, we said thousands of Michael's writings in our library.

We have approximately 5500 writings and audios that are available to you.

Michael: We, and many helpers, have been actively creating this system for about eighteen years. You may want to check out those at a later date. Earlier we had mentioned the six stages that will assist you through your transformation.

The Six Stages in the Abuse Recovery System

    (1) The Memory
    (2) The Choice
    (3) The Experience - Feel to Heal
    (4) The Experiential Roadmap
    (5) Beliefs and Identity
    (6) Clearing Your beliefs

This chapter will cover the first three stages:

(1) The Memory, (2) The Choice, (3) The Experience - Feel To Heal

Adele: I wish that I had these specific steps to follow when I was diligently working through my process!

Michael: And I wish that I had ANY steps when I was doing my process.

Adele: True! LOL!

Stage One - The Memory

How and why you came to the memory

How a memory awakens in an individual varies from person to person. Sometimes it is triggered from an event that you witnessed or something that was said directly to you. Sometimes it is shown in your awakened state or sometimes in your dream state as a vision of some sort.

Sometimes it is a sound, a song or a smell.

Nevertheless, when a memory comes up, things change. They have to. It changes the direction of and the feeling of how you are living. It sometimes explains things that were unexplainable before. Sometimes it may explain why you have been behaving in a certain way or why you were associated with certain people. We can only guess why something is remembered. Maybe a part of your human was ready. Maybe a higher level of you, beyond your human was ready and your human was not ready. Keep in mind that a memory can come from something you know and buried, something you have forgotten or something you did not know you knew.

Adele: Here's my story of how I remembered the memory of sexual abuse.

I was in my freshman year of high school. I made friends with a girl who needed help with a family situation. It involved sexual abuse. Looking back, I felt extremely emotionally charged during the situation. I certainly was not neutral about this topic. I didn't know why it struck a chord with me. I became enraged about the situation. Even at fourteen, I was quite aware that the emotional charge was intense.

That blew over. When I was sixteen years old, I was driving home from basketball practice. I was in a great mood, feeling very alive and loving my life.

While driving, I could feel my grandmom, who had died a couple months earlier. Sometimes I could feel her, like she was right in front of me.

That day, she was more present than ever. And that was the day, my life changed. A memory was made very clear to me, as clear as day. I remembered being sexually abused on three separate occasions when I was six years old.

The memories came flooding in the car like a dam had opened. Flashes of pictures and memories instantly became so clear that I wondered how my mind kept them hidden for so long; memories that I hid so far down for so long that they didn't even feel real or belong to me.

I hid them, lied to myself, but really knew that they were always there and they were mine.

No matter how hard I tried to believe that they didn't exist, the truth was right in front of me. It was clearly me in these memories and I had them all this time. I had just buried them, so I couldn't access them before that day. It was like someone lifted a veil right off of me that I didn't consciously ask for. I guess at some level, I did ask for the memories, because they were remembered by me. It was MY mind that opened the dam.

I pulled the car over and cried. I went from happy to sad in an instant, just from a memory!

"It happened to me, oh my god!" I just kept saying it over and over in the car, out loud as I cried. I sat in the car, crying for a while. The tears just kept pouring down my cheeks and my heart ached.

Why did it happen one this day, when I was sixteen years old? Why at that very moment when everything was going great? I remember saying to myself. 'No Grandmom, take it back."

My whole life had changed in a heartbeat and there was nothing that I could do about it. The flood had arrived. Damn, I couldn't take it back. The damage was done. It shattered my entire life. Nothing was ever the same.

Michael: Unlike Adele, I never forgot my abuse. I can remember before five that there was something not right with how I was raised. Mom didn't feel good to me, she almost felt cruel. Often times, I was repulsed by both my parents and wanted to run but I was too small and had nowhere to go. As I grew older, I learned to find people that would give me what I needed and stayed away from the mad house called "home". Not to mention I felt like earth was this foreign bizarre place where these things they call people were mean and weird. Where was the love?

My mom would often come to my room to check on me. She would start with telling me what to do and what not to do. The harassment and poking at my essence, my core, my being, making sure that I couldn't be still and enjoy myself was endless. She was always about disruption, making sure I did not have any inner peace --constantly disrupting my solitude.

There must have been aspects of her that didn't like this solitude. I believe that she carried these beliefs because she was beaten and verbally abused as a child. From my perspective, the abused part of her did not like to have anyone around her in peace or solitude. Most likely because she couldn't have it herself because of her wounds. Her belief system was based around violence and unrest in the home – so she carried that out.

My mom's approach to almost everything was typically hostile, loud, aggressive, disruptive and energetically violent, mean and downright cruel at times. My mom's abuse was mainly focused towards the male and men. She needed to be in charge and in control to feel safe. She believed there was something wrong with men and that men were dangerous and would hurt you. This was her way of controlling her world and unconsciously trying to create a sense of safety. Once I reached the age of five, I became more completely defined in the men's/male category, not to mention I had a sister who was born. My mom began to bond and isolate the girls against the boys. The women against the men was the unspoken standard in the household.

The abusive patterns and wounds of my mother made it difficult to see and feel any love that she had. I knew they were there somewhere

Over the years, I heard from others that my mom loved me and had good intentions. However, most of my memories were about her cruelty and hostile abusive nature. I know now that somewhere in there inside of her she loved me.

All I had was the memory of the trauma, violence, abuse, disruptions, name calling, cutting words and anger stuck in my mind and the daggers stuck in my heart, **not the love.**

Some people hold on to the love and try to forget the trauma, but that wasn't true in my case.

We, as humans, all do the same things, but differently.

As a child, I fought for my essence and my right to exist!

Both of my parents were survivors of abuse. My dad was equally abused and even told of a time when his father literally picked up boards and would beat him and his brothers. My dad was equally as dysfunctional as my mother, although he was more on the quiet reserved side, he could be quite aggressive or bully his way through situations. My dad was more focused on trying to make the world work and how to work it while my mom was more focused on life not being fair and having to speak up and fight for your life.

Do you see the patterns that I was given?

What horrible things for human beings to have to do just to survive. No matter what level your abuse or traumas are at, they are still abuse and traumas.

Here's a tip:
Never compare your experience to another person's to validate yourself.
No matter how much more horrible someone else's is, yours is still horrible to you.
You do not deserve pain and suffering! No one does!

One of the beliefs that came from my childhood was that people should be kind and nice and if they weren't, I did not want to be bothered with them. For me, this meant that I expected people to be something that maybe they could not be in that moment.

I held on to the thinking that this was a reasonable expectation and that people should be kind to each other because everyone has the capability. This did not take into account their circumstances or their need to grow, which in turn created many disappointments for me as a human being.

Eventually I learned that my expectations were creating many more challenges than necessary; therefore, I have changed my expectations and beliefs. I do not expect everyone to be kind anymore, but I do see that everyone has the potential to be kind and loving and it is up to them to choose it, no matter what has happened to them.

My mother and father died fairly early in my life as an adult. We were not speaking at the time and I did not know of my mother's death until several years later. I now know and for many years have realized how many beautiful gifts she gave me to survive in this world. I do see clearly now all of her wounds and dysfunction, and know that she did the best she could. I have great compassion for her plight, her suffering and her inner misery and I feel the same for my father as well. When you can truly see and understand how and why the people in your life have influenced or created your identity, you can lovingly appreciate all that they have done, even if it was abusive. For me, I developed great character and skills because of the emotional, verbal and physical abuse.

I no longer hold onto any resentment, suffering or negative feelings toward her or my father. I am grateful for my journey, which seems really weird to someone who is not healed/transformed as of yet, but it is true. I have become very wise and compassionate because of what I experienced.

Remember Adele's daughters' reactions to her yelling and how it affected them? That was a very subtle abuse. Remember no abuse is too little. Think back (Feel back) to when your sparkle was dulled. Just touch on that memory.

Exercise V

How was yours remembered? What do you remember?

Write about it from a feeling place. For example: I felt…when…

1. Memory of your Abuse -_____

_____

_____

_____

2. Age -_____

_____

_____

_____

3. What was your life situation like while it was happening? Be specific. -_____

_____

_____

_____

Note: If you still do not remember any or very little of the abuse, or you were just told the specifics about your abuse from someone else that witnessed it, that is okay! Just write some of the things that you feel and believe are a direct result of your childhood trauma. Maybe, write about some of your difficulties, feelings or things that bother you today that may have been from the past.

Stage Two - The Choice

Fear of commitment

Most people who decide to dive into the truth and begin to see all their perceptions or misperceptions about their abuse, begin to worry about who will be affected and how those people will respond to them or what kind of flack they will get because they are revealing secrets.

<u>Are you ready to dive in?</u>
<u>If so, are you worried?</u>

At this stage, it seems to be always about others; people, places and things outside of you. It's typical to immediately go to your mind and ask how others will be affected.

Right here is where you are NOT putting yourself first.

Why don't you put yourself first?
Don't answer that...yet!

Michael: From a very young age, you may have been taught that others come before you and that you are supposed to sacrifice yourself for others. This is a very dysfunctional belief system passed on from generation to generation.

Overall, it is pretty convenient to program others like this because they can use you later when they need to. It is, however, inappropriate and not love!

It Is Your Time!

You Must Come First!

Adele: We, as humans, are sometimes very subtle when it comes to verbal abuse. We don't just come right out and say to our youngsters, "You should sacrifice yourself for others, dear child!"

No, you might hear things like this:

- "Son, you should share that toy with your friend, even though you may not want to."
- "Daughter, just go and play with that other little girl to make her feel better."
- "Give your uncle a hug anyway because you will make him feel bad."
- The comments that dad or mom makes when he or she feels that the child is not their favorite.
- When a parent doesn't feel well, emotionally, he or she clings to their child, sucking the life force out of them.

These things teach the child that everyone else matters before them. You are often even told that it is nobler to sacrifice yourself for others and their needs than it is to care for yourself.

Michael: Oh, hell, they even say it spiritually. "Take care of your fellow man" and of course the ultimate "For God so loved the world, that he gave his only begotten Son."

All of these are misrepresentations. "Take care of your fellow man" means be kind and lend a helping hand where you can. To me, the saying, "For God so loved the world that he gave his only begotten Son" means that Source/ God gave us access to a divine being/master that would help those who would help themselves.

Adele: What do flight attendants say during the safety demonstration before taking off, "Put on your oxygen mask first before helping others.

You will not be able to help anyone if you are not balanced yourself. Alright, maybe they didn't say, "balanced" but I am sure that is what they were implying!

<u>In this model, there can be no self-love or self-care without sacrifice.</u>

This is so ridiculous and devastating to the heart of a child. This in turn creates a dysfunctional adult who allows others to use or abuse them as a way of self-sacrifice or creates a dependent feed/feeder human. This model also not only supports grooming and abuse, but makes you a clear target to be approached by an abuser.

- If you want freedom for your children, never teach them to sacrifice themselves or their needs for another. Ask them what they want. Listen to see if what they want is reasonable.
- Teach them that it is healthy to care for themselves first and then assist others if and when possible.
- Ask them how they feel and about the choices that they are making and why they are making them.

All three of these tools could be taught as early as one years old. It's about teaching our children to FEEL!

In Stage (1) of this guide, you started to allow the <u>memories</u> to come up.

Then in Stage (2), you are deciding to choose this path of awareness and what it takes to heal.

So, now it's time for Stage (3):

Stage Three: The Experience - Feel to Heal

Get ready to retrieve some of your memories again.

<u>You will feel and touch on</u> hurts, guilt, fears and shame, although this time, you are loaded with new understandings and clearer perspectives.

Remember, no judgments! The best advice that we can give you is not to judge. By not judging, it will expedite your process!

<u>Does that motivate you...expediting this process?</u>

It motivated us! We wanted these hurts gone as soon as possible. So, if there was a way to expedite this process, we were going for it!

Trust us, you may forget and judge while feeling these memories, but when you become aware of the judgment, don't be stubborn, just let them pass right by you. Ruminating on your judgements keeps you stuck; instead apply our process. We are hoping that we taught you enough of the basics that judgment will not be necessary, but most of you will do it anyway :).

Don't judge that you are judging yourself!

Michael: Well wait a second, there is only one reason to judge yourself and that is..if it helps you to stop judging yourself! This is what we call positive judgement. Just kidding!

In order to heal, you have to feel your past:

As an adult, you must now relearn that
your primary objective is to care for yourself and that requires feeling.

Never give yourself away or sacrifice yourself for anyone.

Self-sacrifice is not love!

Adele: It might take some time to identify or start noticing when this happens in your life. It's very subtle. Just know that if you really listen to your Inner voice, immediately following the "giving yourself away" thing, there will be a charge. Red Flag: It is a very uncomfortable feeling.

Michael: Giving yourself away only serves others and NEVER serves the Heart!

Why would a child want to give him or herself away?

To please adults or gain something they believe is the only way to get it.

We have to start from the beginning; when you were very young.

Parents can actually deceive their children into believing that they, as a parent, have all the power. Young children have such great trust that they would not know to think otherwise.

Being taught self-doubt or being berated could cause you to turn your abilities and decisions over to someone else. They deliberately set you up so that you doubt yourself and turn your power over to them.

This is how they feed off and control their children. This is when children give themselves away and give their power over to another.

Some children refuse to give their power away, and yell and scream or withdraw and hide. But these tactics have consequences that most children do not wish to feel.

Example I:

Why a child may give herself away.

Adele: Why didn't my six-year-old self speak up or walk away while I was being sexually abused? There had to be a reason! I remember the experience very clearly.

The first time I remember the experience, he was talking to me, as he touched me in a loving way and then the next thing I knew, he was holding my head down to give him oral sex. I must have left my body because I don't remember how he convinced me to put my mouth on his genitals. I was on the ceiling during the act – meaning I was out of my body.

The second time, I wasn't fooled by his loving touch.. Instead, I felt this creepy feeling, which was my first belief about touch - Touch was creepy. I also, felt "bad" from the first experience with him. Second belief – touch is bad.

The third time, I said, "no" but didn't walk away. He touched me with his now creepy hands and convinced me. There wasn't a fourth time because I made sure that I was never alone with him and always stayed far enough away from his body for the rest of my childhood; far enough away from anyone else's body for that matter.

I was so disappointed in him and even more disappointed with myself.

Here is where the spinning began. For me, whenever anyone would touch or was about to touch me, I would move away from them, looking like I was squirming away, or not focused.

I always was very aware of everyone's moves. This was a skill that I developed over time.

I believe that is why I excelled in basketball. I knew where everyone was on the court. It was like a dance when I played basketball, moving purposefully and smoothly with my teammates. I saw the moves, sometimes before they even happened, as my team and I moved down the court, maneuvering in and out of the open positions until we scored.

But I didn't answer the question, did I?

Why didn't I speak up or walk away?

The first time, I was duped. I trusted this person and was not aware of what was happening.

Second time, I knew that I had already done something bad and and I was embarrassed, as well as wrong. If I told anyone then I would have to admit that I put my mouth on his genitals. No way was I telling! I just wanted to bury it.

It was my fault!

The third time, I mistakenly found myself alone in the room with him and then never again!

Michael: Was this a violation of trust? Yes, it was! It's a connection that was used psychically and intuitively to get her to perform an act that she would not have consciously chosen.

If she didn't have that connection with him and didn't have those feelings of wanting him to approve and like her, she wouldn't have performed this sexual act.

Let me try to break this down and explain it to you:

To be clear, Adele's experience was not a 'I'll let you see mine if you let me see yours,' circumstance. I will list the different levels that I feel are associated with sexual abuse.

1. 'I'll let you see mine if you let me see yours,' experience.

2. Adele's experience with her family member was innocent with only the intent to have his experience of pleasure satisfied. Most teenagers who abuse, do it out of an impulse and without planning. Nevertheless, this teenager influenced a child younger than he to satisfied his needs.

3. <u>The Perpetrators:</u> Let's take for instance, a grandfather who deliberately breaks the trust of a child by molesting him or her. He doesn't care at the time that he is doing it. He just wants to satisfy his needs. He may be the nicest human being in the entire world when he is not satisfying his urge. He uses a child's trust to deceive him or her so that he can satisfy this sickness. The child has unwittingly participated simply by being present. Again, the child is innocently available and not looking for someone to do this to him or her, their body is simply there.

The energy and the intent are different when let's say, a teenager is looking to discover himself in his body and thinks it may be easier to have a younger sibling or neighbor take care of his sexual desires.

He may feel that it is easier than trying to do it with his peers or someone older which may probably frighten him. Or maybe when he was young, he was molested by someone older, so he wants to repeat the same pattern. There are so many possibilities

His intentions we believe were not to harm her but to simply serve his own needs. That being the case, he was not intentionally trying to hurt her, yet he was very inappropriate and had no idea of what the effects of that behavior would be. Well, maybe some that do this are aware of the effects of their actions, but their needs were more important.

<u>These types of behaviors leave many scars.</u>

Often times when people do this they have had the experience themselves and unconsciously play the patterning of those experiences out with others. *They don't actually do things to you, they do things for themselves.*

Most children have been affected greatly as any child would. It's all so confusing for the child.

<u>Why a child does not speak up is very important to understand.</u>

<u>So, if this happened to you, how did you deal with it?</u>

Adele: I didn't want to feel my trauma, because of the perceived pain, guilt and shame that went along with the memory. That was how I dealt with it.

During therapy, as a young adult, the therapist told me that it wasn't my fault. My adult mind agreed that it WASN'T my fault because I was just a little girl. As an adult that made sense. How could it have been my fault, right?

<u>Try telling that to your six-year-old mind</u>

My six-year old mind was convinced <u>that it was my fault.</u>

My six-year-old mind still knew the facts and the facts were, I allowed these experiences to happen. I didn't scream or run, nor did I hit or bite him to escape. I stayed and because I stayed, that made me guilty. I was embarrassed and ashamed for giving a thirteen-year-old oral sex. He held my head down yes, but I could have resisted in some way as a six-year-old. I had legs to walk away, but I didn't, so it was my fault. I was given a voice. I could have said. "No!" I wasn't physically forced down. So, because I didn't walk away and didn't say "no", my perception of the experience was that it WAS my fault.

<u>Do you see the dilemma?</u>

This is often how children think and feel; I have listened to many children and adults who have been sexually abused. Logically, if a child clearly knows that it wasn't their fault, the act wouldn't be such a problem, therefore the abused person wouldn't have any issues, right?

But this almost never seems to be the case. Even knowing this, people commonly feel like they are at fault somehow.

The piece that assisted me with my freedom from this type of responsibility was the fact that I was there, present, during the abuse. I was physically present for it. If I wasn't there, it wouldn't have happened. Therefore, the only thing that was on me was the fact that I was there innocently, the rest was on the abuser.

<u>I owned my experience when I admitted that I was there and nothing was my fault;</u> I didn't do anything wrong, even if I was an <u>*unwitting*</u> participant. If I owned that I was present, then I could forgive myself for putting myself in that position. I didn't need anyone else's forgiveness but my own.

Also, I went outside of myself to seek approval and satisfaction from others. I wanted to be liked by others. I believed that I needed to please others, and yet I disliked others who harmed me, at least from my perception; that put me in quite a quandary.

I was mentally and emotionally reaching outside myself to others in order to acquire some sense of self and yet, at the same time, I wanted to be invisible. That is just simply not possible!

Michael: Most people don't like to think that they have participated because then that carries even greater guilt and shame for participating in an incident that they have judged as a wrong and then have judged themselves as being wrong for having done it.

Wonder why people avoid feeling?

People don't like to admit this because if they do, then they cannot be a victim and many people hang their identity on being a victim. Being a victim allows you to avoid your own responsibility for choices you feel bad about and it brings sympathy and pity, which also allows you to avoid your feelings, in fact it avoids your transformation/healing.

It is not to say that you don't deserve to mourn the loss of your innocence, just don't hide behind victim-hood and then suffer your whole life.

To admit that you <u>unwittingly</u> participated consciously or unconsciously, on any level, brings about such guilt that it can actually destroy the ego personality of the individual, if you are not prepared to take personal responsibility for your life and realize that you are a participating creator in your life experience, even if you do it unconsciously.

When you realize, or admit that you have <u>unwittingly</u> participated consciously or unconsciously, it is not to feel guilty, bad or wrong but rather to recognize that you were simply a participant. All this means is, like we said earlier, that your body was present; therefore, it makes you a creator or at least a partial creator of the event.

In the long run this will empower you to realize that you create everything you experience. With this knowledge and wisdom, you can recognize that you don't need to blame anyone else for anything and that somehow on some level you have <u>unwittingly</u> participated and created the event for the wisdom of your soul.

Even though this may not make any sense to your human self, sometimes in the bigger picture it makes complete sense because you are a divine being that just has forgotten who you are.

You have forgotten that you are a creator of your experience.

So, as you are so involved in learning how to be a human, you tend to forget you are a creator. I am saying this to you to remind you of the creator that you are. This will then empower you to change your perceptions and your beliefs.

You can then create the experiences you wish to have rather than be a victim to the experiences you had and have judged through misunderstandings and misinterpretations.

Adele: Just because my body was present, doesn't mean I asked to be abused. By circumstances or due to my need for love, I was circumstantially present. It was not my fault as a child. Owning that I was there and I didn't walk away and absolving myself from my guilt and shame for being there is one of the most loving acts that I did for myself.

The guilt, shame and wrongness for being there is what trapped me in the pain of abuse.

This was a huge revelation for me!

The guilt, shame and wrongness that I was there and didn't walk away or say, "no" WAS what kept me stuck and frozen in my six-year-old mind.

<u>Not The Act Of The Abuse</u>

It is NOT about the Act of the Abuse

To truly be free from this pain of the abuse, you have to understand that it's not about the act of the abuse.

<u>It is not about the act of the abuse,</u>
<u>Rather it's about the beliefs that you have formed from the abuse.</u>

This is such an important sentence and it assisted me in going to the next level!

When you truly understand this statement **at its core,** it will change things for you.

Again, it's not about the act of the abuse, it's the beliefs that you create in your life that haunt you, poke at you, and cause an uncomfortable or painful experience.

If you created the belief, guess what…you can undo it! Let me say it again!

If you created these distorted beliefs
Then you can UNDO them!

Do you hear me?

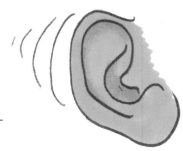

Listen!

OPEN UP YOUR EARS!

<u>This is what you have to understand and then
eventually accept within you!</u>

All your life, you may have been told that you didn't matter or maybe that you weren't good enough or you were not tolerated, directly or indirectly. Whoever was telling you that was saying it for their own distorted reasons. Remember: People don't do things TO you, nope…they do things for themselves, from their own patterns.

Concepts #16

People don't do things to you, they do things for themselves - **Michael Cavallaro**

We, as human beings, do not do things to others, we do them for ourselves.

Even when the action taken is toward another, it's out of your need to gain something. Financial, emotional or material, there is a perceived benefit, either consciously or unconsciously. It doesn't matter if it's logical or irrational; there is still a perceived gain.

Your beliefs put you in the position of being done to; you energetically attract events because of your beliefs. Understanding this allows you to realize that there are no victims, there is only the fulfillment of beliefs. People unconsciously like to be victims because it releases them from personal responsibility for their beliefs, choices and actions.

Change your beliefs and change the way the world shows up around you. This will help you change what you attract so you can resonate with other, more preferable, life experiences.

Remember all human beings do things for themselves, not for or to others, including YOU.

<u>Let that sink in, a bit!</u>

This is true for no matter what kind of abuse. If you do not admit that you were present during the event, you are not fully owning your experience.

<u>This is a very subtle form of denial.</u>

And if you are in denial, how can <u>forgiveness of self</u> possibly work? If on one hand you are saying, "It happened but I wasn't there, and I forgive myself," you are then saying, "I am forgiving no one because no one was there."

Over the years, we have worked with many individuals who have experienced all types of abuse. Most people psychically and emotionally leave the body during traumatic experiences or deny that the experience happened. If you do either of these, how can you truly heal?

<u>You must learn to be safely in your body
and own that your body was present during the experience.</u>

Anger

How Do You Deal with this Feeling

Adele: When I was young, I rarely showed my anger, oh but it sure was in there. If I was upset, pissed or irate, I held it in.

Here's what I had to admit and also learn to move beyond my anger:

- I was so angry that I gave in to a family member's desire, a thirteen-year-old stupid boy who wanted what he wanted when I was six-years-old, because I didn't want to speak up and say no.

- I was so angry that I was so naïve and stupid that I fell for someone else's manipulation (thirty-year-old groomer when I was fourteen years-old).

- Because of these experiences, I was angry at myself for being so stupid, dumb, gross, dirty wrong and bad.

<u>Being angry at myself was not the only problem; judgment was equally important.</u>

Who would want that nasty, angry feeling to come out and show its face. NOT ME!

When these feelings of anger were remembered, and acknowledged by me, I couldn't find a category to place the feeling. Remember the controlled experience that we mentioned earlier? How would I control this anger? I controlled it by suppressing it and became busy. I spun and also caused drama in my life, mixed in with a little numbing abuse.

- Some are able to hold in these emotions.
- Some allow them to passive aggressively seep out a little at a time.
- Some constantly act out these emotions in their everyday life.

The only option for me was to leave these emotions in my body - space out, numb myself, join many activities, sports, clubs and have LOTS of friends.

<u>That was me in a nutshell.</u>

Everyone appeared to love the thirteen-year-old abuser, so they never would have believed me; when I did tell a few people when I was a young adult, most didn't believe me.

Here's what I had to admit and also learn:

- I was angry that he didn't admit it, when I told him that he sexually abused me.
- I was angry that I was rob of the chance to have a safe, intimate experience about touch and had to carry around the confusion about touch most of my life.
- I was angry at the fact that I felt that the human body was gross, dirty and scary.

My experience with the thirty-year-old groomer who displayed love and peace that I mentioned earlier was similar--he was also loved. He was cool, groovy and spiritual and seemed to others to be all about the love. There was no way that I was revealing what happened. Although, if he reads this guide, he will know who he is.

Here's what I had to admit and also learn:

- I didn't even see the underlying intentions that ran alongside the love - Neither did anyone else.
- I was so angry and embarrassed that I was duped.

- I regretted that I didn't expose him sooner, so other young girls didn't have to experience what I went through.

The experience that I mentioned earlier about the priest, he was also loved and appeared cool to many. He also had that spiritual and cool persona. Even though he worked on grooming me and stayed in touch with me for twelve years, he fortunately didn't succeed with me. But he did succeed with some of my girlfriends, as well as other boys in my catholic community.

Here's what I had to admit and also learn:

- I was so angry that I thought he was my friend for such a long time.
- I was so hurt that the man that I remembered helping me after my father's death in the seventh grade was a fraud and had other intentions.
- I felt stupid while reading the letter that had been written by this pedophile priest, realizing as an adult that it had all these other meanings embedded in it.

NOTE: I am happy that this priest is locked away and will not groom and abuse another child again.

<u>I always felt that I owed these individuals something.</u>

<u>This is very common.</u>

The fact that I owed them didn't even make sense back then. But nothing rarely makes sense when you are emotionally *charged* in a belief system.

<u>I owed them because they were nice to me.</u>

That sounds silly to me now. I believed that I didn't have the right to speak up and tell them how I felt.

At times, I had this incredible amount of hate for them, but then I would stop the anger because I judged the anger that was inside of me. I believed that anger was cruel and not love. Anger was intense and not kind. I judged the suppressed anger within my own family. Remember if I judged it, I had to have had some within me and I did.

Michael: Everyone is afraid of anger, at least at first. Anger is only the surface of the wound. The wound is underneath and at the core of the anger. Fear causes you to use the anger to keep yourself from being wounded again. So it is the wound and the hurt, maybe even grief, sadness, or loss. However, the wound is at the core. Fear then follows - The fear of having to repeat it or re-experience it again. Then the anger which is the repulsor, the rebuffer the chaser away of danger and further wounds. And yet the anger that which is perceived as the protector actually is that which anchors you to the wound and the feeling that is underneath. When you remain angry you choose unwittingly to say; that experience is part of me, it defines me. Also understand that the wound is anything or experience that you perceive or define as having hurt you.

The energy of anger repressed creates a perspective of grief or hopelessness and that energy turned inward destroys the desire to feel and numbs the heart. In that no feeling state, depression exist as life being void of happiness, joy or desire to encounter life. Which then causes a withdrawal from the world and an inner isolation and ambivalence. If it is tuned into apathy or hopelessness there is a completely different energy and experience of giving up and quitting life.

Adele: Instead of admitting my judgment of anger and exploring why I was angry, I suppressed the anger and often would say, "Maybe it was my fault that I didn't say no."

<u>It wasn't my fault!!</u>

Do you hear that??

I was young. I shouldn't have had to even be in that position to have to say no!

You shouldn't have either.

- The thirteen-year-old should have known better
- The two grown adults in counseling positions knew better but didn't care.

<u>They all wanted what they wanted.</u>

I saw only what I wanted to see. I had so much anger for myself that I allowed this to happen.

I did, in fact, participate in these acts of sexual trauma, but not in the way, you typically think of the word, "participation."

<u>The internal conflict was sometimes unbearable.</u>

<u>Dealing with the feelings was very difficult, but I did it.</u>

<u>Remember:</u> The process requires you to only touch on the feelings that you fear and perceive as scary and intense, not get swallowed up and drown in those feelings.
<u>It was when I allowed the memories to surface, chose to do whatever</u>
<u>it took to transfomrm/heal, and then resolved these feelings through the process</u>
<u>that I could see all three of these individuals in a new light.</u>

<u>Some of the things that assisted me:</u>

- Judgment of Self - seeing my own patterns.

- Forgiveness of Self - understanding that I was victimized - but never a victim - allowed me to move to the next level.

- Knowing that because I created these beliefs, I could undo them.

Again, If I created it, I could UNDO it

I love this one! It changed everything for me! The way I saw, experienced and interpreted everything changed. It was amazing. If I created it, I could UNDO it!!!!

<u>Owning your experience for freedom!</u>

<u>If I create an experience, then I can UNDO it, if I so choose!</u>

<u>I have the power.</u>

<u>Ownership equals freedom</u>

<u>Ownership:</u> Unwitting participant (consciously or unconsciously), again, *simply means that you were present.*

<u>Keys to Freedom:</u> If you were present for the act, you created it; therefore, you can undo it!

Breaking of the Trust

Breaking of the trust is most painful when the trust is abused by someone.

But people misinterpret the act that broke the trust as the problem. They then focused on being a victim of the act rather than the breaking of the trust, the loss of innocence or the utter shock of being used. The focus becomes centered on the act and not the inner aspect of the person that gets traumatized. It is the inner part of the person that gets traumatized and is not about the event at all.

As an <u>unwitting</u> participant, you created this experience, you allowed it simply by being present. If you forgive yourself for being there, then <u>you can fully detach from both your wrongness and the abuser.</u>

Adele: This is what changed things for me. This is what we call "accepting and owning your behaviors", the concept that we mentioned earlier. Some of you may want to put down this guide because you will refuse to believe that you participated in the abuse in any way, shape or form.

You spent all this time, your entire life, trying to figure it out, trying to place these feelings and behaviors and memories in a box, so you could live a normal life.

<u>I know. I get it.</u>

Even if you were as young as six, *you participated,* consciously or unconsciously.

I had to ask myself, how did I benefit from this behavior?

Deep down, which I couldn't admit at first, I thought if I just did what he wanted, pleased him, kept it quiet, it would be done and over with. It could be buried and wouldn't be noticed or brought up. That was easier than speaking up or fighting. People that have been sexually abused get these two statements.

Think about that. As an adult, that sounds so ridiculous. <u>Rather than speak up, I will just give myself away.</u> I understand that today, but back then, not so much.

Today, I see it in so many people. People give themselves up in conversations, business meetings, classrooms, sports, it goes on and on, not to mention, what goes on behind closed doors.

Here's the other piece to this: If you want something from a situation or from someone, you will also give up yourself. For instance, let's say, you wanted love from your abuser or didn't want them to be mad at you. Even if you wanted love, that was still wanting something from the abuser even if it was reasonable to want love. It's a trade-off.

This was very difficult for me, especially with the groomers. I wanted love. I wanted attention from them because I didn't love myself enough to realize that it was my own love that I needed;

<u>My own love was all that I needed.</u>
So, unwittingly, I gave myself away to get the perceived love that I was searching for.

<u>Again, that concept was a tough one.</u>

When you begin to own your behaviors, and forgive yourself what you participated in, things start to change.

If you created this, you can undo it!

I created this.
I am the one who was there, present.
I was the one who gave myself away, so I created and allowed it.
But guess what?

If I created this, I could undo it!

This is where change started to happen for me.

I literally felt the shreds of guilt and shame fall right off of me as I worked through this process

Forgiving myself on all levels (because it was also lifetimes of these patterns) consciously and unconsciously, for having these feelings of fear, guilt, hurt, shame and even pride. Iit started to break free and be released from my very being.

Remember when you own your behaviors, you can let go of this act and see it as a benign experience, meaning, it's not good or bad.

Concept #17

There is no good or bad, there is only toward Source or away from source – **Michael Cavallaro**

Good and bad are merely judgments based upon preference. Life is filled with benign events that you give your own meaning. You are merely judging what your beliefs tell you that you are seeing or experiencing. What is a tragedy for one person can be a gift for another.

In this case, toward Source or away from Source means becoming conscious, rather than falling or staying asleep in the illusion of life or dysfunctional belief patterns. When you see life as a larger picture, the tragedies of life are not so tragic. The truth is that you never know what the big picture is for anyone, and there may be a purpose that you are not aware of. Seeing this way is the difference between a child's perspective and an adult's perspective.

The same event can have a different meaning and not be as awful when you know the deeper reason for the event. It is not to say that you do not or cannot have compassion or understand the struggles of others; you just see them from a different point of view. And from that point of view they are no longer tragic; they have great meaning. And in that meaning, are many lessons and resolutions that the blind man cannot see. Remember that life is a learning experience and people often see what they do not want to learn as unpleasant. But this does not actually make it unpleasant. It is only perceived as unpleasant because of the person's resistance to learning or perception of the experience.

Adele: I simply made a choice to get something. In my case, it was to obtain love and to be love or what I thought was love.

<u>You will no longer ever, and I mean ever,</u>
<u>have to give yourself away for anyone or anything.</u>

<u>All you have to do is love you.</u>
<u>Do you truly love yourself enough to do what it takes?</u>

Well, that is what we are going to find out!

Chapter Six
SUMMARY

- The Memory

- The Choice

- The Experience - Feel To Heal

- When it comes to abuse, it is never about the act of the abuse, however awful it was, but is about the perception of the abuse/trauma. The trauma is about the feelings, perceptions, interpretations, meaning, and beliefs that you made about the act of the abuse.

- Resolving these is what will get you to your freedom! In the end, it is only about being free of the limitations and pain that the abuse/trauma created for so you can live an enjoyable, even happy life. No Blame! No Shame!

- You have to forgive yourself, on all levels, either though consciously or unconsciously, for feeling guilty, shameful, dirty, bad, wrong, disgusting, hateful, etc. These are the feelings that stop you from the happiness that you so deserve.

- You may not be in a place to forgive yourself, just yet - don't judge it.

- You will get there if you keep an open, honest mind and heart.

- **Concept #15** *We Chase what we believe that we do not have.*

- **Concept #16** *People don't do things to you, they do things for themselves.*

- **Concept #17** *There is no such things as good or bad, there is only toward consciousness/Source or away from Conscious/Source.*

- <u>**Exercise S:**</u> Lion's "Walk Your Talk" Design

- <u>**Exercise T:**</u> What do you still desire but do not chase?

- **Exercise U:** What do you desire and still chase? Things that you believe that you do not have.

- **Exercise V:** Remembering a memory of an abuse from a feeling place.

- Let's do a quick recap on what you have learned intellectually about beliefs, belief systems, perceptions and patterned behaviors.

- Belief systems and desires create and manifest challenges in your life; they can be both conscious and unconscious.
- The conscious ones are easy to identify; but the unconscious ones are the ones you must begin to learn about and identify in order to change your life.

- You are creating everything in your life through your beliefs, perceptions and patterned behaviors. It is like you are a magnet and only those situations that relate to your beliefs and patterns will be experienced or brought into your life.

- You can only experience that which you believe in or believe is possible.

- By understanding this, it sets the stage for you to change your belief systems and eliminate beliefs that are preventing you from creating and experiencing the life you want.

A simple belief system

Let's say you grew up with parents who believed that money was scarce, and you must work hard to earn just enough to get by and pay the bills. You, as an adult, let's say, carried on this belief unconsciously. You work hard yet never seem to get ahead or have extra. When you do seem to get ahead, your car suddenly needs repair, you get a speeding ticket, or an unexpected bill comes in the mail. That expense eats up the extra money you have and now you're just making it again.

<u>Start to keep track of your patterns</u>

This would be a belief system at work and a way you keep attracting the same life situations in order to fulfill a belief such as: "You can't get ahead or have extra."

Ready to learn how it works?! Here goes!

Get ready for Chapter Seven!

Chapter Seven

Your Roadmap to Healing

Dottie (Short for Dorothy)

By now you should have an understanding of the basics.

Don't feel you need to understand everything in depth you have learned thus far. As you work the process, these understandings will gradually begin to sink in. You may want to refer back to the first six chapters for some clarification when needed.

You will definitely want to repeat the two exercises (that we have provided in this chapter) each time you are faced with another internal challenge.

Think of this process as a web of answers, it's just not linear.

We are trying our best to make it as understandable as possible.

The Seven Steps to Freedom

So, once you:

- (1) Know that you are unhappy where you are and have the desire to change
- (2) Have an awareness of what makes you unhappy
- (3) Accept responsibility for your behaviors and choices
- (4) Understand the payoff or the perceived benefit of your behaviors and choices.

Then you should be ready for the

Seven Steps to Freedom (5)

Understand and see how you created your life situations (beliefs) and how this works.

Here's where it gets fun!

This is where you will watch your patterns unfold right in front of your very eyes.

Stage Four: The Experiential Roadmap

Before we explain this next exercise, we would like to tell you how this <u>Experiential Roadmap</u> was created and why it is so helpful.

Adele: I used to believe that putting men in categories was my own creative way of coping; apparently, I was not alone. This form of categorizing was a very common occurrence for most.

For me, categorizing allowed me to keep track of the males that were in my life. I could be in a room full of strangers and be able to categorize them for my perceived safety. This categorization alerted me to anything that was unexpected..

I lived a controlled experience (See chapter One) inside a shell that appeared very easy going from the outside.

For instance, I could go from business woman to bubbly, personable Adele, in seconds and then back again. You could say that this was a well-developed skill. I excelled in the business and social world. Maybe on the outside it looked like freedom, but it was not at all on the inside.

<u>This was not true freedom; this was not living a life, free from limitations.</u>

My skill was the ability to control my outside world. For instance, I prepared and educated myself on who was who. I could walk into a room and categorize the males in minutes.

- First, I immediately put my feelers out.

- Second, I used the categorization process. I categorized in my mind:
    a. The perpetrators.
    b. The males who would disregard me and could hurt me emotionally.
    c. The males who could take from me.
    d. The males who were safe.
    e. The males who would honor me.
    f. The males who I could control.

From my experience, most abused people are very controlled and calculated, staying in their minds so they can avoid feeling. If you were abused sexually and/or emotionally, verbally or physically, as a child, you may have develop these types of awareness skills. You may have been very aware of everything and everyone in a room, office or sporting event...possibly to feel safe.

In this exercise, you will have the chance to categorize the individuals in your life so that you can sort out each of the thoughts, beliefs and patterning that you have created, that prevented you from relaxing around others - a life free from limitations.

<u>Imagine that? Truly relaxing around others!</u>

Before you do this, you have to be open and get blame and shame out of your way.

Blame and Shame

Until you finish blaming, you cannot move on to your transformation. Feeling blame and shame will hinder your growth in <u>understanding how you attracted/created your life situation (beliefs), and how they work.</u> You often feel justified in your blaming, which causes you to be in shame and repeat the same patterned behaviors of victimhood, guilt and powerlessness.

Two Examples:

- Your wife is watching the children and one of them gets hurt. You become angry and berate her for not being more aware, blaming her for the accident. You later realize that it was not really her fault and it could have easily happened on your watch. It happened because your child was simply being a child and adventurous and got hurt. No one is really to blame.

- You blame your father for you being such a fearful person because he was always afraid of everything and never taught you to be courageous. Later to realize he did not have the skills and you felt ashamed of yourself for being so mean to him growing up.

In order, to move on, you *have to* get past the blame and victimhood! We understand if you are not there yet. We can guarantee you that there is no transforming when you are in blame or victimhood. When you are in blame, you are still in the past, when you are a victim, you are in the past and your healing is in the present.

Concept #18

There is no blame, things just are - **Michael Cavallaro**

We, as humans, love to blame, for in doing so we are able to deny our responsibility in how our lives play out. Blame is a handy tool to avoid our own issues and responsibility. Taking responsibility often means doing something we would rather not, so we tend to avoid it. If someone or something else is the cause, then things that happen are outside of our control and we do not have to change ourselves.

This is so much easier than looking within at our own flaws or errors, for we all hide from our sense of wrongness. Wrongness is a common human core belief. Even if we are willing to look at ourselves, we still have areas that we avoid consciously or unconsciously. If you think you do not, we can guarantee that your programs are at work.

This blame may be verbal or mental; it is the same, either way. It doesn't matter if it's seen or unseen, it still produces the same effect. To the universe there is no blame, things just are. This we call is-ness, because it just is.

Blame comes from victimhood; remember you are not a victim and if you feel like or think you are one, it is only because you were taught to be one or believe you are one. Change this belief and change the way you experience and create life.

We don't expect you to resolve the blame and shame within you immediately, but be aware of these two words as you work this process. They most definitely will slow you down at times.

When you do come upon this (and you will) our suggestions are that you read parts of the first six chapters again, as well as, ask yourself how are you benefiting from being a victim and what is it about yourself that you are not looking at that is causing you to judge and blame.

Exercise W

The Experiential Roadmap

- First, we will <u>present an example</u> to make it easier for you to complete the exercise.

- Second, we will <u>provide you with 4 charts</u> for that example, that will include sections A through E.

- Third, we will provide you with <u>detailed instructions</u> for the exercise.

- Fourth, you will have the opportunity to <u>fill in your own life experiences</u> in 4 new charts, as we did with the example.

Example:

There was a boy who was raised by a dad who appeared to be angry, short-tempered and impatient. The boy felt that his dad disregarded him from his perspective, but this was what he felt as a result of his dad's behaviors and words. His dad was physically sick most of this boy's life which may have caused some/most of the frustration in how he was treated. As a result, the boy felt unsure of himself for most of his life.

<u>Note: It didn't matter if his dad was sick or not; what mattered was identifying accurately how the boy perceived the experience.</u>

At age eleven, this boy was sexual abused by an older cousin. Before he was sexually abused, he felt safe around his older cousin. He liked and looked up to him as well. He never was the same after he was abused. It changed his life.

At age twelve, this boy was groomed and then raped by a priest. He was perpetrated, betrayed and spiritually abused. He became numb after that day, as well as developed a great distrust towards males.

At age thirty, he finally found a woman who loved him. After about five years of marriage, he started to withdraw, isolate and avoid closeness and touch. His wife then became distant and asked for a divorce which caused him pain. He felt betrayed because she wasn't honest and didn't even warn him that she was unhappy. He shut down and became depressed.

The Experiential Roadmap

Trauma/Abuse Experience
Chart #1 – Parental Figures

A.
Who Was Involved?

Dad

B.
**What did you expect or hope
of their relationship to you?**

Teach me to participate and prepare me
for the world to, things, correct me,
make adjunctions, explain my
misperceptions, love, respect and honor.

C.
How were you involved unwittingly or otherwise?

Hyper, annoying, loud, spatial issues

D.
**What did he/she do or what did you
perceive them to do, specifically?
Physically, emotionally, sexually, verbally,
energetically or spiritually.**

Disregarded, shunned

E.
**How did this individual's behaviors
affect you in childhood or as an adult?
What are the adverse results/effects?**

Feeling unsure of himself

The Experiential Roadmap

Trauma/Abuse Experience
Chart #2 – Youth Perpetrators Under 21

A.
Who Was Involved?

Cousin

B.
**What did you expect or hope
of their relationship to you?**

Safety, trusting, loyal, fun

C.
How were you involved unwittingly or otherwise?

Participated in the act of sexual abuse

D.
**What did he/she do or what did you
perceive them to do, specifically?
Physically, emotionally, sexually, verbally,
energetically or spiritually.**

Sexual abuse

E.
**How did this individual's behaviors
affect you in childhood or as an adult?
What are the adverse results/effects?**

Robbed him of a normal sexual
perspective, the start of distrusting males

The Experiential Roadmap

Trauma/Abuse Experience
Chart #3 – Trusted Professionals

A.
Who Was Involved?

Counselor, Coach, Priest, Teacher

B.
What did you expect or hope of their relationship to you?

Advice, teaching, mentoring

C.
How were you involved unwittingly or otherwise?

Misinterpreted his intentions, made it about attention

D.
What did he/she do or what did you perceive them to do, specifically? Physically, emotionally, sexually, verbally, energetically or spiritually.

Groomed him, perpetrated, spiritual abuse

E.
How did this individual's behaviors affect you in childhood or as an adult? What are the adverse results/effects?

Became numb, Distrust humans

The Experiential Roadmap

Trauma/Abuse Experience
Chart #4 – Partner

A.
Who Was Involved?

Partner

B.
**What did you expect or hope
of their relationship to you?**

Honesty, listener, open

C.
How were you involved unwittingly or otherwise?

Unaware, not connected, afraid of touch, avoided closeness

D.
**What did he/she do or what did you
perceive them to do, specifically?
Physically, emotionally, sexually, verbally,
energetically or spiritually.**

Secrets that she didn't tell him earlier
that she wasn't happy, pain, betrayal, hurt

E.
**How did this individual's behaviors
affect you in childhood or as an adult?
What are the adverse results/effects?**

Distrust relationships, destroyed trust,
lack of communication, shut down.

Chart #1 - This boy had a dad who was supposed to love him unconditionally, model love, **teach** me, appreciate and respect his existence, not **disregard and shun** him.

Chart #2 - At age eleven, this boy was sexually abused by his older teenaged cousin who was supposed to be safe, not sexually abuse him.

Chart #3 - Counselors, spiritual leaders, and coaches were supposed to advise, educate and assist; not groom, **perpetrate** and influence this young boy (now fourteen) until he was convinced that he belonged to them, owed them and believed that he had no choice but to have sex with them.

Chart #4 - This boy grew up and married a woman who was supposed to share her feelings, not **keep secrets** about not being happy and cause him **pain by telling him she wanted a divorce without any warning.**

Why would these people do such inappropriate things?

We don't know the first thing about what was going on with these individuals. We don't know their backgrounds, life experiences, belief systems, patterns, childhood and how they became the way they are today. It is a fact that all of these individuals had their OWN core programs, family patterning and belief systems.

<u>As adults, we get it, everyone has challenges, but growing up, as a young child getting abused, like this boy, not so much and so we interpret our experiences the best we can.</u>

Some potentials/possibilities as to why these individuals did these things:

Chart #1 - Let's guess that the boy's dad had cancer and was really struggling, and the boy was very hyper, had no spacial awareness and was constantly annoying the dad when he needed quiet. Suppose he appeared to disregard his son because he found him annoying or maybe his dad was disregarding him because mom made it clear to him that her son belonged to her and dad was to stay away from him.

Chart #2 - We could speculate that the older cousin had a rough time growing up. We could guess that he was molested by a priest/neighbor when he was young.

Chart #3 - Suppose the priest perpetrator was sexually abused himself and then joined the priesthood. He was then taught a system how to abuse young girls and boys in the seminary – a system that involved targeting children, like this boy, from poor or emotionally, traumatized families (such as a death in the family) because these children were vulnerable and an easy target. Suppose this system really exists and it is used to teach how to abuse and get away with it. (That is another truth and possible story for another time and another book.) Maybe the priest meant well when he said he could help this boy with his sadness of his father's death before he molested him. Maybe the priest knew that he could fill the void of the love that the boy desired so desperately from his dad. Maybe the priest didn't care, and he was simply grooming him, and he was completely aware of the fact that he had already been abused and he was a perfect target for a future abusing.

Chart #4 - Maybe his wife didn't mean to betray her husband and cause him pain. Maybe her family patterning was that men were not emotionally available; therefore, she married him because he matched her patterns.

We don't know for sure about any of individual's background, for we are not them. We can only speculate. Some of them had no clue of the long-term effects that it had on this young boy. Some may have known and not cared. We don't know, again; We can only guess.

Are you ready to try?

Instructions:

A. In Chart #1, (Parental figures) Write who was involved in your experience/abuse/trauma, in section (A,).

B. Write in section (B), what you expected or hoped of their relationship to you?

C. Write in section (C) how you were involved or participated unwittingly or wittingly?

D. Write in section (D), what he/she did to you or what you perceive them to do, specifically? Physically, emotionally, sexually, verbally, energetically or spiritually.

E. Write down in section (E) how this individual's behaviors affected you in childhood or as an adult? What are the adverse results/effects?

Apply this same process to: Chart #2, #3, #4 **using** Sections (A), (B), (C), (D) and (E) instructions, if applicable. <u>Some boxes you may leave blank, if they do not apply to you.</u>

Be sure to double check the Key below, for Parents could also apply to a uncle and a trusted professional counselor could apply to a neighborhood parent.

KEY for the Charts:

#1 Parental figures – parents, guardians, foster or adoptive parents, uncles or aunts.

#2 Youth Perpetrators under 21 – siblings, cousins, neighborhood teens, older students

#3 Trusted professionals and spiritual leaders – counselors, coaches, teachers, pastors/priests, neighborhood parents, managers

#4 Partners – husband, wife or partner/love

Remember:
Try to write how you feel versus what you already
know in your mind about your story.

The Experiential Roadmap

Trauma/Abuse Experience
Chart #1 – Parental Figures

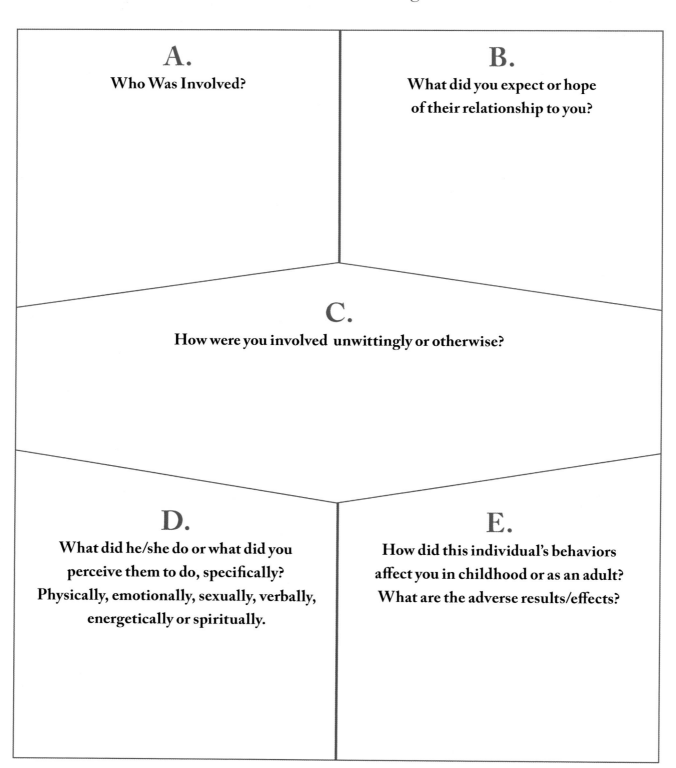

A.
Who Was Involved?

B.
What did you expect or hope
of their relationship to you?

C.
How were you involved unwittingly or otherwise?

D.
What did he/she do or what did you
perceive them to do, specifically?
Physically, emotionally, sexually, verbally,
energetically or spiritually.

E.
How did this individual's behaviors
affect you in childhood or as an adult?
What are the adverse results/effects?

The Experiential Roadmap

Trauma/Abuse Experience
Chart #2 – Youth Perpetrators Under 21

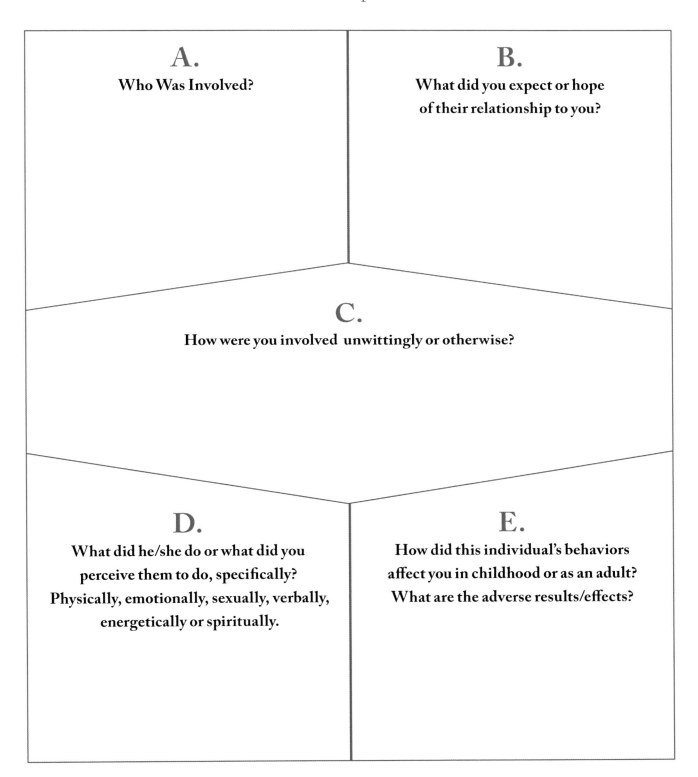

A.
Who Was Involved?

B.
**What did you expect or hope
of their relationship to you?**

C.
How were you involved unwittingly or otherwise?

D.
**What did he/she do or what did you
perceive them to do, specifically?
Physically, emotionally, sexually, verbally,
energetically or spiritually.**

E.
**How did this individual's behaviors
affect you in childhood or as an adult?
What are the adverse results/effects?**

The Experiential Roadmap

Trauma/Abuse Experience
Chart #3 – Trusted Professionals

A.
Who Was Involved?

B.
What did you expect or hope of their relationship to you?

C.
How were you involved unwittingly or otherwise?

D.
What did he/she do or what did you perceive them to do, specifically? Physically, emotionally, sexually, verbally, energetically or spiritually.

E.
How did this individual's behaviors affect you in childhood or as an adult? What are the adverse results/effects?

The Experiential Roadmap

Trauma/Abuse Experience
Chart #4 – Partner

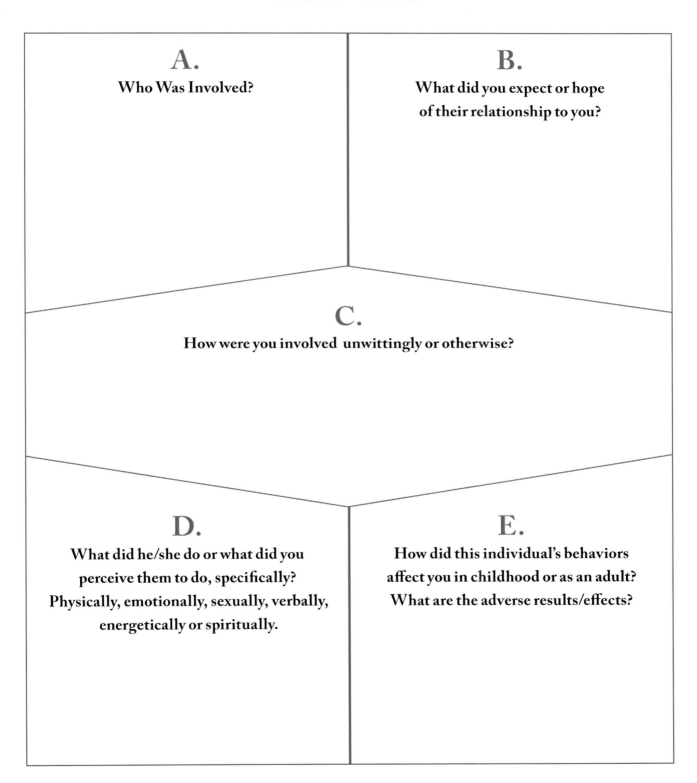

A.

Who Was Involved?

B.

**What did you expect or hope
of their relationship to you?**

C.

How were you involved unwittingly or otherwise?

D.

**What did he/she do or what did you
perceive them to do, specifically?
Physically, emotionally, sexually, verbally,
energetically or spiritually.**

E.

**How did this individual's behaviors
affect you in childhood or as an adult?
What are the adverse results/effects?**

This exercise was not to judge the people who abused you, but rather to begin to **Understand and see how you created your life situations (beliefs) and how this works - Seven Steps to Freedom (5).**

Seven Steps to Freedom (6)

Understanding where these beliefs come from

Adele: Again, it's always best to start at the beginning...your beginning!

Michael: Okay Glenda!

Adele: Yes, Glenda!

The character, Glenda, from our novel, *Searching for OZ,* a creatively, written, fictional account of a personal journey (My journey) of self-love & finding love, set on a creative platform with the Wonderful Wizard of OZ theme, that conveys healing information for anyone with a history of trauma.

Glenda pops in and out of Dorothy's, life, the main character; as some of your helpers do on the other side!!!!

Michael: Read it! It's a great story! Marvel is the most interesting character.

Adele: Marvel (Michael) is very cute!

Michael: Dorothy (Adele) is pretty sweet herself.

The Journey Inward

Adele: Going inward is the only path to being free from limitations; the things that we have been talking about throughout this entire guide.

Michael: What the hell does "going within" even mean? LOL

Going inward is simply touching on some of that perceived pain that we just spoke of.

To simply "Go inward" and feel pain is one thing, but to have a process that you can work through and dismantle the hurts, guilt, shame and fears that are in there, is another.

First things first!

There needs to be room for YOU…in You!

There needs to be no one in you, but YOU!

Would you agree?

Often times, it seems too scary, painful or too overwhelming to "be or live" inside yourself, but that should not be true anymore. Now you know not to judge what you perceived, created and lodged in there. Now you know, that what's in you are simply family patternings, distorted thoughts and some misperceived beliefs that you made up about yourself.

Now let's empty out anything that is about anyone or anything else. Nothing belongs there but you!

You will have to empty out that old stuff!

Concept #19

Empty your cup so that you may be filled – **Michael Cavallaro**

You cannot fill a full cup. Whatever you pour into a full cup will spill out. In the same way, you cannot use new information without changing your existing beliefs; old patterns will still govern your life. Empty your cup so something new can fill it.

Rid yourself of old beliefs so there is room for new ones. If you believe you are always right, then there is no room for error. If there is no room for error, then there is no room for change. Without change, there is no growth.

We are human, so there will always be error. None of us will ever be perfect if we are defining perfect as without flaws.

This journey does not end; it is an eternal growth process.

In Search of your Inner Wizard

Who IS the Wizard that you are looking for?

You silly! YOU and only you!

Yes, you are the Inner Wizard!

And you have a VOICE!

Michael: An Inner voice! It will take some time to really embrace this. It will be really important for you to be focused on you and only you and your experience.

As we said before, you will want to blame others, make up stories about the pain and go outside of yourself to see other perspectives. The only perspective you need to focus on is yours!

That is, if you want your freedom!

What is freedom?
Freedom is the ability to create what you want to experience
rather than experience what your beliefs and programs create.
Having conscious choice!

Wait! You still want your freedom, right?

Of course, you do!

Your Ego

First, you must understand the basics of your human ego for the next exercise. You will need this information to better understand the Four Building Blocks of Beliefs and Identities.

There is so much talk about the Ego. People say things like;

- The ego is being egotistical.
- The ego is only an illusion but very influential.
- At the deepest level of existence, there is no separate Ego.

- The ego was created out of fear of God.
- I am my ego
- I need my ego
- Your ego is obnoxious
- You have a big ego
- The ego must be eliminated

For our purposes, this is how we define the ego.

Concept #20

*The Ego is a Tool – **Michael Cavallaro***

The Ego is a required navigational tool for all human beings to exist in this world.

It is not to be destroyed or suppressed. It is to be loved, understood, used and operated with your consciousness as a way to experience this world. Without it, we would not be able to function here on Earth.

With it, you could flourish. it is to be understood that the ego is to serve the heart but in most cases, the ego is either in charge of a person's life or serving the mind. If the ego is in charge and/or serves the mind, you are living a life based on your patterns and beliefs. which brings about all of life's typical and difficult challenges.

The ego only does what it has been programmed to do. This programming took place while you were unconscious as a child. It is up to you to reprogram it so you can experience life the way you want.

So in other words, your ego is the aspect of you that allows you believe and perceive that you are separate from Source and your bigness while living the human life.

Identity

The Identities/facades/personalities that you create are in fact the curtains that you place in front of yourselves. They are the makeup or masks you place on your ego which you hide your essence behind.

The identity is who you are taught to believe you are and you assume that information to be true. Beliefs and roles that you assume to be you. (ie. I am a mom, a farmer, a teacher.)

So in other words, your identity is who you perceive you are, based upon all the information that comes from outside of you and that you believed and accepted as defining you and have made it your truth.

- **Ego** = Separation

- **Identity** = Roles, qualities and characteristics that you believe define you!

Your identity and ego will be present throughout all <u>Four Building Blocks of Beliefs and Identities.</u>

<u>It is time to look behind your identity and facade</u>

<u>It is time to look behind the curtain to find those beliefs that you made up about yourself!</u>

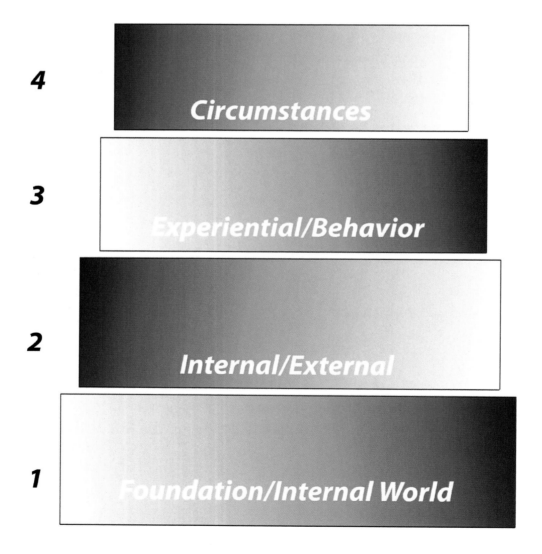

The Seven Steps to Freedom (6)

We will now give you a better understanding where your beliefs come from

Michael: Now let me show you how to trail back to your beliefs and identities.

When you trail back to find an identity, you typically start at **Block Four** *where you are and what you are experiencing in current circumstances. Here is where you currently create your situational circumstances.*

Then you begin to trail back through **Block Three,** *observing and understanding what was causing you to have these behaviors and experiences. Here is where you played out your beliefs and actually how those beliefs were displayed.*

Then in **Block Two** *you projected your beliefs onto others to find out where you belong in the world to see how you belonged or fit in. Here is where you decided how you were going to carry out what you believed.*

Block One *is your Foundation of the inner parts of you. This is where you had actually created these beliefs and Identities Here is how an assumed truth began. Your human ego was born here and in the womb.*

Stage Five: The Four Building Blocks of Beliefs and Identities

The four building blocks of beliefs and identities has been designed this way to demonstrate different blocks that build and rely upon each other.

Block One being the foundational base which supports all the other blocks, which in turn leads to Block Four your current circumstances in adulthood. Each block going up is how you began and then graduated into a full-fledged human being.

- *First, we will explain the details of each one of the building blocks along with an example, so you can see a model of how and why it's necessary to trail back to find your own. It will show you what fits in each block.*
- *Secondly, there will be plenty of detailed explanations of that example.*
- *Thirdly, after the explanation and the example, you will have the opportunity to fill in your own by using the same format.*

This writing will lead you through a process which will assist you in trailing back to where you first started struggling and where you first decided to believe something about yourself; therefore, forming an identity of who you thought you were.

Block One - Foundation of your Internal World

The Foundational Block One is where your identities and beliefs are created.

It is basically, the inner aspects of You in this lifetime.

The first block is your <u>inner world only</u>! It does experience the outer world but this is the inner development of your identities and your beliefs. Yes, you have multiple identities. This is where your foundation begins, based upon your family members and home environment.

- *A single parent*
- *The two main parents/guardians*
- *Siblings*
- *Anyone that is considered to be in your immediate family unit or primary caretaker*

This foundational block is from conception to about six years old, give or take, depending on the individual.

This block is where you start to feel, experience, witness and decide who you are, based upon your perception and interpretations within your home and environment.

Here is where:

- *You had no control and barely any discernment skills.*
- *You had none or barely any cognitive skills.*
- *You may have developed some cognitive skills toward the end of the stage, but not enough to say that you were a conscious human being doing them.*
- *You were basically a little child, running around the world and were pretty*
- *unconscious – on autopilot. You were kind of bouncing from one person's energy to another person's energy, reacting or acting based on the family programs with a dash of soul memory.*
- *You didn't really consciously know all the levels of what you were doing or why you were doing it.*

Block One Example:

There was a girl who grew up in an large family. She was born two years after her brother and when she turned one, her mother birthed twin girls. A year after that her mother had another girl. Between the ages of one and three years old, the first part of the Foundational Block One, this girl wanted her mother's love and attention.

Her mom was too busy with the others to give all of them the love that they deserved. She paid close attention to what her mother noticed and what she didn't.

She found one way, through a behavior, that would win her mother over and make her stand out so mom would pay attention to her. She became her mother's helper. She even assisted her mother with her older brother. She had found a coping skill that would get her something that resembled love - behavior approval that she perceived of as love..

As long as she did what her mother asked, her mother *seemed* proud of her and appeared to love her, at least that was what she told herself.

By the time she was five another baby appeared on the scene and she began caring for the baby changing diapers, entertaining her and watching over her as her mother did other things. She was also responsible for the other children and even during the middle of the night feedings for the new baby. By the time she was seven her mother left her alone to watch the children while she ran errands and such. She watched her mother's frustration grow as she watched another child join the family.

As the family grew, her mother's temperament began to turn into impatience, anger and sometimes rage. She was reprimanded almost every time a sibling got out of line.

As each new child arrived, she became more and more attached to her sibling's safety, as well as responsibility for their well-being. She continued to hold her feelings inside and stepped into the strong identity of the leader of the siblings, even motherly. She felt alone, unhappy and unsure of herself, but the only thing that she was confident about was her identity as the leader of the siblings.

The following are some concepts that turned into beliefs for this girl:

- My family doesn't understand who I really am - a girl that was craving love..
- I can't make any mistakes.
- I should know without being told

- I should be able to observe and understand
- If I was good enough I would just know
- I need to be perfect.
- I am/need to be in control.
- I am an authority.
- I am not loved if I am useless.
- I believe that I need to give up my needs and desires for others.
- I come last/others come first
- I must manipulate to be satisfied
- I am loved if I take care of things.
- I am loved if my mother approved of the way I took care of things
- I am on-guard with family/reactive to family behaviors.
- Some family siblings disregarded me for my bossyness but it was the only way that I could do my job to keep the kids quiet
- If my siblings did not obey, we would be punished
- I needed to keep my siblings safe from punishment
- Being Disregarded became abandonment.
- I became not important and didn't matter unless I was caretaking
- Watching over the family was my purpose in life
- I am not lovable.
- I am not good enough.
- I must sacrifice for others
- I must keep others happy
- I must do what others want
- I am not important
- I am not seen
- I am only valued as part of the family
- I am separate from the family.
- I am nothing without the family

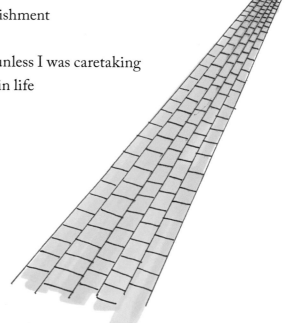

This belief system created the girl's identities. Then at six years old, she had to figure out how to cope with these beliefs and use them. By this time, they were accepted/assumed truths which turn into behaviors.

So, whatever she needed to do she would do to gain acceptance, tolerance, or to be regarded, and feel perceived love. Based upon how her family acted with each other, reacted to each other and acted with her, she started to form an idea of who she was in that environment. She then related that perception to who she was in the world and to who she was as an individual.

So, because of the family patterns, she began to disregard herself and abandoned her own self, which then led to behaviors associated with her belief systems, so you see, all these beliefs and identities are developed in this Foundational base.

Remember this foundational base is your inner life.

Michael: *It was where your identities and beliefs were created. It's your foundation for your inner world, pre-cognitive as well as some cognitive, it supports and drives who you believe you are or are supposed to be.*

This foundational base includes all the sensate feelings and discoveries of your introduction to this life. It is the place to find the answers to most of your autopilot beliefs, identities and behaviors that are sometimes not explainable.

Now, add an emotional or physical trauma to your belief system, create a judgment, and it intensifies your whole experience.

Keep in mind that block one is your inner life – that which goes on inside of you, and in the next few blocks we introduce your outer life – that which goes on outside of you; your environment.

Continuing with our example of the girl.

The girl witnesses mom shaking her little brother in frustration. Her heart drops. Fear sets in. Then mom and dad rage at each other, throwing things at each other. The girl immediately gathers the siblings and brings them to a safe place. Both incidences, cause a perceived trauma as well as, create fear of violence and of mom and dad.

The awareness of beliefs, patterns, and core programs is necessary.

Core programs are the source, then the core patterns are formed, creating and supporting beliefs, perceptions and judgments which in turn support thought and then create behaviors.

The behaviors support the thoughts, the thoughts support the beliefs, the beliefs support the core patterns which support and sustain the core programs, which then in turn, create beliefs and so on and so on endlessly. They all feed each other perfectly which is what we call – a feed-feeder system.

The core program is a code that tells the energetic core patterns what to form. It forms a frequency grid to allow the beliefs to manifest in a person, consciously or unconsciously, which then gives the person access to the guilt, fear, shame, etc. (EFI), which then manifest physical and emotional display.

Creating everything that you experience or bring it to yourself means that some conscious, semi-conscious, or unconscious aspect of you is bringing an experience and vibrational frequency into your conscious awareness so that you can resolve or change a belief system or core program that is not love.

Most people think that bringing it to yourself comes from you being aware of what you were creating. This is not true. Ninety percent of the time, things that you create are brought to you by your unconscious/soul memory or spirit for you to consciously experience in your conscious awareness/everyday life in order to bring it out of your unconscious for you to grow.

These distorted beliefs eliminate your chances of living free from the hurts and pain that most people talk about.

Every human being has the core programs, core patterns, beliefs, thoughts, behavior system! It is one of the reasons why you are here working through this book; to master that system!

In this Foundation Block One you are observing and imitating everything and everyone. You are experiencing life, as well as feeling and judging what is going on around you.

This is where you start to believe some of what you are seeing, hearing and feeling, as truth. But the truth is one of these are yours, you only claimed them as yours.

Remember, beliefs are assumed truths; those things that you were experiencing could have been true or not and most likely were misperceived.

Remember, identities began forming at birth. From birth until typically six years old, you are in the process of forming an identity based on another person's reality and then eventually you create/form an identity.

Identity is the character, qualities, perceptions, beliefs, personality, appearance and/or expressions that make a person seem to be who they are.

I am a sister, a daughter, a mother, a father, an aunt, an uncle, a fireman, a counselor, a democrat, a republican, a salesman, a contractor, a woman, a man – identities are confused with roles. All of these are roles not identities!

But after repeating them day in and day out for many years, you begin to believe in these roles as who you are and then they too become identities. The true self is lost by programming and repeated behaviors being accepted as who you are. Thereby creating a belief of who you are and the loss of inner connection to the "True Self".

**Roles are chosen behaviors based upon beliefs that
when repeated over and over typically become identities.**

Identity is derived from the Latin word identidem, meaning "over and over,"

The fact is your identity is a repeated behavior or way of thinking based on a belief system that eventually becomes a way of perceiving yourself. This then becomes habit and renders you "unconscious" while believing you are the roles that you have chosen to play. Hence you lose consciousness and begin to act on autopilot the way the belief system and identity calls for at any given moment. At the time, the belief system becomes an identity you are living "unconsciously" as there is little "pure consciousness" of you present, yet you appear to be conscious of what you are doing. The fact is that you are unconsciously living a preordained appearing conscious lifestyle but have lost your connection with the "true conscious self"!

What a mind bender, right??? Wow was that a load of information! Take a breath or two and begin to read again.

A role is a behavior that you choose to fulfill or not.

Everything you believe about yourself is part of your identity. Identities are simply belief systems. The qualities of an identity, as in our earlier example, I am not good enough, I was abandoned, I need to self-sacrifice, I am intolerable and/or I am disregarded, are what became of the girl, as a result of her beliefs and identities becoming real and her disconnection from her inner self.

Would a lovable person be abandoned? No, if someone left a lovable person who believed that they were loveable, that loveable person would most likely want to know what was wrong with the other person leaving and why did they do it. It wouldn't be because of the loveable person; it would be because of some other reason.

Ninety-nine percent of the time, a child blames him/herself for what is happening, in order to fulfill the belief that "I am not lovable." At this point, a child typically believes that love comes from the world around them unless they are taught differently. So, anytime, their environment changes, the child asked the question, "What is it about me that makes me not lovable." Then whatever associated beliefs about their identity exist are then supported and become thoughts, experiences and reality.

The experience of the girl in our example; As long as she believed that love came from the outside world, she was limited and had to earn it.

Limited to the whim of others and no true experience of her own therefore she had no control. The problem lies with the misunderstanding that as a small child your physical needs (like being cared for, being fed etc.) equals love. And that is then transferred mistakenly to the external world once you can care for yourself.

Children need total physical care until around the age of five or six. The child misinterprets physical care as love, yet in most cases, parents give both simultaneously which adds to the reason for this misunderstanding. This misunderstanding is not the child's fault. However, this misunderstanding becomes a belief and a truth which then distorts the child's expectations and perceptions about love and physicality and later sexuality.

This often turns into sexual issues and misinterpretations in the teen and young adult years. Between the raging hormones and emotional needs that are based on the earlier misunderstandings and misinterpretations, teens and young adults now act out sexually and project their need for love and connection onto the sexual act and mating process.

Michael: Need a cup of tea or maybe some oxygen?

Adele: LOL! Yes, there are still three more blocks to go!

We felt that it was important to spend more time on the Foundational Block One because it's connection and importance to the remaining three blocks. Block One is the foundation on which your whole life is built.

Internal/External

Block Two - Foundation of Your Internal World

Block Two is when you project your created identity onto the world to experiment and see how you belong or fit in.

It is basically, you projecting your beliefs onto others and trying them out for size.

The Internal and External Life Block Two is the time when you project your created identity of yourself onto the world, to see how it works. How it is tolerated by others and what responses you get.

Block Two Example

So in the earlier example of the little girl, she now becomes around seven years of age. She begins to play with her inner world, as what she has learned thus far, and practices her new identity with the outer world. She interacts with other people and interprets what she knows about herself from her inner and outer worlds' responses.

So, in that, she starts to take all those beliefs that were created in her foundational base and starts to practice living those beliefs to see what works and what doesn't.

She meets the neighbors and immediately wants to take control. She is constantly looking out for other people's safety. She is serious and there is no time to play. She organizes games, makes sure no one cheats or is unhappy, all the while losing sight of fun or happiness for her.

At that point, the girl starts to use some of her behaviors on herself. She judges herself, tries to live up to everyone's expectations, sees her failures and incompetencies and on and on it goes.
This is called "self-abuse".

By the time she is ten, she becomes seen as a second mother, by her siblings. Mom treats her as an equal, as long as she does what mom wants her to do and she knows that mom is the boss.
At this point, she is so confused with who she is and who she should be that anger and frustration, as well as, fear and hurt, begin to bleed through her attitude and behaviors.

So at this Inner/Outer life, Block Two, you are projecting the created identities from Block One both onto yourself and the outside world. It's your experimental world. You ask yourself, does this work? Does that work if I say this, if I make a funny face, if I behave this way or that way? Can I compensate for the parts of my foundation that do not work or can I elaborate on my foundation to show everybody how magnificent I am, how much I deserve love, how special I am in order to get what I believe I need?

Know that Block One is where the ego is developed. This ego is unconscious. and tells you that you are separate from others and human. Block One is the foundation block where the ego is without conscious awareness of self — it is what we will call the basic human ego.

Block Two is where the conscious awareness ego starts to get developed. Block Two is when the ego begins to develop in a more conscious fashion. It then becomes the conscious awareness ego, the part of you that is aware of your human self but not of the higher aspects of your consciousness. It begins to try things out that it has witnessed at this stage as a form of experimentation.

This Block Two will probably be at work into the teenage years and beyond depending on the maturity of the individual.

In Block Two you are practicing with your identities, this is where you discover how you participated with family and friends and neighbors, preschools and what works and doesn't. You also discover how you try to avoid the emotions that you started to feel from the foundation Block One in order to continue the experiment.

So here at Block Two practicing to see how you can stimulate, manipulate and create responses from the external world to get the feelings inside of you to prove and sustain the identities and the beliefs that were created in the foundational Block One.

Block Two is not just projecting outward but it is the experimental stage where you use the beliefs and identities that were created in Block One to get your "sea legs" in the world.

These include questions like:

- How do I make the world work?
- How do I fit in?
- How does the world respond?
- How do I use myself with others and without others?
- What gets me what I want and what does not?
- Can i get my needs met and what is required?

The following occurs in Block one but it is more intuitive and less conscious or not conscious at all in Block One.

It is in Block Two that these things become evident to your conscious awareness. It is here that you often decide and have validated if you are good enough, lovable or worthy based upon the reactions you get or perceive you get. It is here where the identities and personality gets a permanent foundation and become the "you" most people will know

At this stage most people turn over their worth and value to the external world and abandon themselves.

You then project this created identity and decide how this experimenting works or doesn't work so you can take that into the next level of your existence, Block Three.

It is at this stage (Block Two) where you're really forming who you believe you are and who you believe you are supposed to be so you can go off and live it in Blocks Three and Four.

At this point you are deciding who you are: a quiet person, a bad person, a happy person, a kind person and so on. It is where you decide on who the the human self, is going to be. Roles begin to develop and solidify in this block. You practice the roles that go along with the created identities. They will then seat fully in Block Three.

Continuing with our Block Two Example of the girl.

With the created beliefs of self-sacrifice and giving herself away from her *Foundational Block One* beliefs, she begins to practice and project out to the outer world what she believes about her inner world and what the outer world has confirmed.

How does she make her world work knowing that this is who she is? Well, she practices it on neighbors, preschool and grade school friends, teachers, church leaders, and teammates in sports. She tries to make sense of the world through her projection. She asks herself, How am I and how do I fit in the world – bringing her inner world of beliefs and limited self-perception to the outer world all the while desiring outerworld confirmation of her inner world.

She may have thought the following:

- How do I give myself away to be accepted?
- How do I project my beliefs and identity and look for the world to respond. If it doesn't respond the way it's supposed to feel, she'll place herself in another situation until she finds that feeling that tells her she is in the right place, however incorrect that feeling is.
- She practices projections. People begin to respond to whatever she puts out there, so she displays her focus and leadership skills. Adults take a liking to her and use her as a helper.

In Block Two, Identities are solidified. This Internal/External life Block Two then is supported by and supports the foundational Block One.

You've learned who you are at Block One the foundation. You've practiced who you were and tested it and found what worked and found what didn't work during Block Two.

For the most part you've established a familiarity with this identity and these beliefs and you become "comfortable in your skin". You interact with the world through experiences and behavior and now the belief, this is who I believe I am is established. This is called the human ego/identity. The human ego/identity knows who and what you are or are supposed to be.

Remember Block Two is where you become your conscious awareness, the part of you who is aware of your identity as a fact or truth. The Block One is the basic ego just knowing that you're separate.

So now you're interacting with the world and in interacting with the world you're going to find friends, family and relationships that all support Blocks One and Two. Do you see how they all are based on each other?

This is created in the shape of a Mayan Pyramid or a multilayered cake because the blocks are smaller as they go up and become foundationally less important. Foundationally meaning that the bottom block is most important to the ego/identity of the person, the foundation where everything was established and the higher up the blocks you go, the less important and more flexible for change.

We now begin to move up into the Experiential and Behavioral Block Three (external), the interacting realm, which interacts with the world at large. Where, the previous stages were primarily family (internal) and a small amount of the world (external).

Block Three - The Experiential/Behavioral World

Block Three is the behaviors that you act out and how they are displayed while you perfect your outer world identities.

It is basically the place of observing, understanding and identifying with your behaviors.

The Block Two is where the identity is practicing who it believes it is. Block Three is perfecting the same.

This process is very important to young children in seeing where they fit in based on what they believe from the Block One foundational level. This Experiential and Behavior Block Three starts to become less important and more autopilot as people age.

During Block Three, people are interacting with the world through experiences and behaviors. They start to develop friendships. They join groups and clicks. The clicks that they have joined all support the Blocks One and Two.

So, they could be in a band, in sports or they could be writers. They could be talkers or shy, it could be anything. Within each one of the blocks are the EFI (Energetic Fields of Influence) and the EFI in each one of those blocks are associated with the belief system you established, so if you are a shameful person then the two common EFI are shame and pride. These qualities are developed and attached to your identity which becomes your truth. This will be different for each person yet very similar.

Block Three Example

During Block Three, she is doing more of the same, as she was in the previous two blocks. The only difference here is that she is refining her identity while practicing the beliefs she holds about herself.

At this stage, she seems to be very sure of herself on the outside and follows orders but lacks original thought but inside she is terrified of making a mistake and being disapproved of.

She continues behaviors that work and changes those that do not. She is perfecting her identity.

At the same time, she is creating more wounds and misinterpretations that she must then adjust her identity to.

During this block, the hormones kick in and trigger a whole additional set of changes. The hormones activate parts of the brain and disrupt logic, all while the individual is trying to establish an identity. This usually adds to the confusion and instability of the individual's emotional status and affects the ability to discern and sometimes behave properly while the patterned identity develops. Also during this block a new aspect of the child is integrated.

Circumstances

Block Four - The Situational Circumstances, The Current Now Block

Block Four is where and how you choose to carry out what you have learned from the previous stages.
It is basically, your experience in the situational circumstances of life. At this point you are at the pinnacle of adulthood.

Here you are completely interactive with your Outer/external Circumstances in your life, Block Four. It is where you're tied into, attached and bound to the world. You believe everything in the blocks below and it is 90% forgotten, and yet everything below supports you as an adult. Your adult self is the face of "who I am" as a human being. It is the showpiece of all your labor.

That 90% form the lower 3 blocks is still there, you just don't remember it. If it wasn't there, your identity would collapse. You are busy presenting your face to the world and all that information is now in the subconscious automatically supporting every bit of your identities.

Back to our example of the girl:

Block Four Example

She believes the only way to survive is to be everything she has created and feels locked in, even imprisoned.

She becomes the Head Nurse at a large local hospital; close enough to home in case her family needs her. Known as being very prompt and focused by most of her peers and the hospital board, she is responsible for the direction, organization and strategic planning of the nursing department facility. Her job description is to evaluate the nursing staff performance and work closely with the upper management and external agencies in the organization of the patient care.

Of course this was a perfect career for the girl who never gets married because of her packed schedule. It was here that she felt right at home being in control, leading a group, as well as caretaking. Because she was neglected as a child during her foundation block, she felt that her worth and value came from these qualities.

So her compensation to the Block One lessons was to be kind so that others would accept her. (The caretaker comes from the rejected child. The caretaker then presenting that kind face to the world would be seen as a wonderful person, but in reality, 99% of caretakers are dysfunctional and are taking care of others to compensate for their wounds.)

She leads a staff of 75 people, leading is an innate skill by now, making sure that everyone is in line. Her boss loves her because she rarely makes mistakes and everything is under control.

This is adulthood. This is the circumstances of life. This is where situational things happen, you fight with friends, you have career issues, you have child raising issues and whatever else goes on in your adulthood. You are living the circumstances and the face/ego/identity of you is handling it, but this face/ego/identity is based on your previous stages/blocks all of which is based on other people' belief systems.

This is the human ego.
- *This is false ego because the basic ego in Block One is based on just being separate.*
- *Block Two is who am I practicing to be for others, you are developing the who am I to others belief systems, the conscious awareness.*
- *The false ego at Block Four is the belief in the limited/programmed self and its acceptance while being valued by all the other egos. This is called "Self Esteem".*

Self Esteem is the measure of how the the false ego feels about itself!

If anything in Block One changes in adulthood, the whole tower topples or at least wobbles. In other words, your identity comes into question or falls apart.

So, Block Four is a false ego because who you believe you are is based on Blocks One, Two and Three, which were all created from a belief system either passed on or perceived and derived as truth. But either way, the belief system is false and made up by the generations before this one.

If you did not learn that abuse was possible during the foundational Block One, it would not happen in any of the other blocks. Because it would not exist, therefore it could not be experienced. If you were in a perfectly healthy situation and your Block One was pure healthy consciousness, you would have no sense of abuse, rejection, giving yourself away or any other negative qualities.

So even if nothing happened up to six, nothing abusive could or would happen. It must be supported by the lower blocks, belief systems and identities that were passed on and created in order for it to be possible. The only other outside chance of it happening was if at a soul/spirit level it was desired or required for some sort of growth. But otherwise this would not be possible, it would not be in your consciousness.

This is why we designed the block metaphor this way because at the Circumstances Block Four is full adulthood. So, anything that changes in the blocks below Block Four (beliefs, core patterns etc.) challenges the adult ego/ identity.

You can't change too much of the foundation too fast. If you do, it could be devastating to the person and their identities. If the ego or identities feel too unstable, it will go back to Block One to find something, some belief or experience to prop up the adult ego/identity so they can remain functioning and look normal.
But if too many changes take place too fast, the adult persona starts to collapse inward onto itself and can't hold this block/identity. So now the ability to function in the world starts to fall apart.

Then their internal and external interpretations start to fall apart and eventually their whole identity starts to crumble. And you have this tower that basically starts to collapse inward to the middle down to their core programmed self at Block One.

So the idea behind this process is to change consciously by trailing so the adult self is understanding the changes and thus learning skills and new perceptions to stabilize it with no critical collapse, thereby allowing the identities and ego to make conscious shifts while remaining functional and stable. _

When you get to be the human adult, Block Four, there is a choice to return home or what we call; Return to Love. You can remain for the rest of your life as this functional/dysfunctional person/false ego.

<u>Where nothing ever changes except you do learn how to</u>
<u>manage all the different dysfunctions and basic life coping skills.</u>

But that my friends is for another book.

Exercise X

Now that you have been educated
on the blocks, we want you to give it a try.

The Four Building Blocks of Beliefs and Identities
Your Process

Situational Circumstances - Block Four
(Typically between the ages of eighteen/twenty-one until now)

1. What are the current circumstances and experiences in your life that are not working for you now?

_____

_____

_____

_____

_____

2. Describe how this plays out in your life.

_____

_____

_____

_____

_____

Experiential and Behaviors - Block Three
(Typically between the ages of thirteen - eighteen/twenty-one years old)

1. Why do the things that you identified in Block Four bother you?

_____

_____

_____

2. What thoughts, feelings and behaviors did you experience when bothered by your circumstances as a teen?

_____

_____

_____

3. Where do you remember seeing or having the same or similar feelings in your childhood or with your birth family?_

_____

_____

_____

Internal and External - Block Two
(Typically between the ages of seven - twelve yrs. old)

1. Did you do these same behaviors as a child? Please describe them.

_____

_____

_____

2. If those behaviors weren't the same, what did they look like?

_____

_____

_____

3. How did you benefit from these behaviors?

_____

_____

_____

4. What identities did you create from these experiences?

_____

_____

_____

5. How did you try out/test/project these identities on others?

_____

_____

_____

Foundation – Inner - Block One
(Typically between the ages of one - six yrs. old)

1. Where does your current circumstance mirror your childhood?

_____

_____

_____

2. What experiences did you have in childhood that cause you to feel the same as in your current circumstances?

_____

_____

_____

_____

3. Please describe the following:

- What events or behaviors did you observe as a small child?

_____

_____

- What was modeled to you?

_____

_____

- How did people treat you?

_____

_____

- How did you feel about the way you were treated?

_____

_____

- What traumas/abuses did you experience?

_____

_____

- What happened to you?

_____

_____

- How did you feel about your family?

_____

_____

4. As a result of what you identified in question (3), what beliefs did you create about yourself and your world?

_____

_____

_____

_____

5. How did you carry/act out those beliefs or decisions within your family?

_____

_____

Exercise Y

List some of those beliefs that you have discovered about yourself.

_____

_____

_____

_____

_____

_____

_____

_____

_____

_____

_____

_____

_____

_____

The most important information that you need to retrieve is the belief.

It is imperative that you find the exact wording and frequency of how you lodged that belief/perception into you.

This is why we say that you created it! You lodged it in there in a very distinct way; therefore, you are the only one who can undo it!

It's as simple as that!

The skill here is being able to feel/sense the exact wording and/or frequency. It's like finding the right key that turns the tumblers in a lock in order to open it.

Anyone can learn to trail with our process but it's the individual that can feel/sense the words and the frequency behind the words that will make the difference in the clearing.

Understanding the impact that these beliefs had on your life.

Do you really feel and understand the impact of these beliefs?

We cannot express enough how deep and far reaching these beliefs affect you, your life and those you connect with. These beliefs invade every aspect of your life!

These beliefs have created difficulties, as well as limitations in your life and have direct impact on your current circumstances and outcomes! They also contribute to your decisions, actions today and everyday. To let these beliefs go undiscovered is like asking for someone to control you without having any say.

Beliefs make or break lives. We now want to get into beliefs a bit to show you how and why your beliefs are the majority of the problem. We also want you to remember,

Your Beliefs Are NOT You!!!

Your beliefs are assumed truths that operate either from your conscious awareness or your subconscious. These beliefs are ideas and perceptions that you assume to be true without question and believe to be an absolute truth.

You base your life, decisions, behaviors and reactions on these assumed truths without question. Why do you do this? Because you do not know any better and believe your beliefs to be true!

You get the majority of your beliefs from your parents and your environment, (please...no judgments on your parents). Those beliefs are approximately 90% established by the age of six.

Most of these beliefs are generally inaccurate, coming from the perceptions of you as a small child. Along with distorted messages and beliefs received from your parents and surroundings while you were young, when you did not have the ability to discern what was happening accurately.

- From those assumed truths, you make decisions in your life that create the circumstances you experience.

- You see life through a set of predefined filters.

- Decisions about what you like and don't like, about the type of person you want to be, the type of people you like and the type of relationships you're going to have, are decided from these highly inaccurate assumptions believed to be truths.

- Then the events that follow and your interpretations of what you believe those events to mean, based on your assumed truths, create your experience and perceptions in life. Can you see how this can be very limiting and inaccurate?

- Are you starting to understand why we at least have to consider reevaluating where our beliefs and where they come from?

- Add to this – a bit of emotion and boy, do you throw gas on the fire now!

- Emotions throw all reason out the window and the assumed truths become fact! Fact now becomes unquestionable and you now know what you are seeing as absolute truth and respond accordingly!

- Although, what if you are wrong. How would you know? It all feels so real.

- You are so sure that what you feel is real. What if you are wrong? Now what?

<u>That is why you MUST Question Everything!</u>

Identifying your belief is just not quite enough.

Chapter eight will explain.

Before we move on to Chapter Eight, let's summarize this chapter!

Chapter Seven
SUMMARY

- **Concept #19:** *Empty Your Cup*

- **Concept # 20:** *Ego is a Tool*

- **Seven Steps to Freedom (5)** - Understand and see how you created your life situations (beliefs) and how this work.

- **Exercise W:** The Experiential Roadmap Design

- **Seven Steps to Freedom (6)** - Understanding where these beliefs come from

- **Exercise X:** The Four Building Blocks of Beliefs and Identity.

- The skill is feeling the exact wording and frequency.

- Anyone can learn to trail with our process but it's the person that can feel the words and the frequency behind the words that can make the difference in the clearing.

Chapter Eight

Transforming Your Life from the Inside Out

Stage Six: "Clearing Your Beliefs The Transformation"

Here's where the last and final step comes in! Even though this is your final step, you will continue to repeat this process when issues come up.

But we feel that the Seven Steps to Freedom (7) is necessary in order to permanently end the cycle

Seven Steps to Freedom (7)

Clearing the beliefs

Clearing the beliefs should include 4 things:

1. Become conscious of the belief.

2. Become aware of the thoughts that you have associated with the belief.

3. Become aware of the feelings that go along with these thoughts and belief.

4. Use a process that diffuses or dissipates the belief.

In clearing the beliefs, you do not need to clear each individual belief. You will find that there are groups of beliefs that belong to one central feeling.

What this means is this:

- We have found that there are clusters of beliefs that can be cleared together instead of doing each individual one to expedite the process.

- In order to make real permanent change, you must have some sort of belief changing process!!

- You need this to assist you in order to reset your subconscious mind and begin to shift the neural pathways in the brain.

This is imperative in order to completely rid yourself of old limiting beliefs, otherwise everything you have learned up till now is just a mental and intellectual experience!

Real change permanently occurs when you combine this new wisdom with the/a process that actually shifts the energy/programming in the body, mind and soul memory. Our process does this.

Belief Change Package

There are a few other reputable methods that we have heard of that are available also. But of course, we are partial to our own.

Our method has been developed, tried and tested over a fifteen year period with hundreds of people with all varying types of beliefs, backgrounds and religions and we are quite confident it will work for anyone who applies it properly.

You not only have this guide to assist you in trailing back to your beliefs and Identities, but an entire support system that will back you up:

- We have the Searching for OZ video-online and introductory and comprehensive course, individual coaching sessions, that you can register for to assist you in a deeper understanding.

- We have facilitators and therapists who are trained in this process to work you through your blocks and challenges on an individual basis or small group setting.

All of the above are available at: www.adeleandmichael.com and www.livingconcepts1.com

To use our method specifically to change your beliefs, please visit our website above and download the following:

1. The Belief Change Package – This is the foundation for everyone to change beliefs. To use this belief package, email us at adele@adeleandmichael.com requesting the download and we will send you the link.

2. The package is normally $350. For those of you taking the Searching For OZ introductory or comprehensive courses, there is **NO Charge!**

3. We do however ask that when you have used the belief package as instructed, that you please send us a donation $ of what you feel the ability to eliminate your beliefs is worth. This allows us to continue our work of helping others. Thank you!

Please keep in mind that this process and Belief Change Package is <u>the Intellectual Property of Adele and Michael LLC</u> and is not to be share without the written permission of Adele and Michael LLC.

You may have another process of your own to clear the beliefs. <u>If so, go for it! Do your own process</u>. But if you find things not dissipating or constantly returning please come back, try ours! Please reach out to us and ask for assistance.

Second level courses are also available:

The Human Mastery Course – Part I & II and III tele-classes – these three levels are an in-depth study of how we work, live and have created our identity as a human being. The where and why of everything in detail.

RE-Entering the Matrix

Here are a few concepts that will assist you with Re-entering the Matrix - meaning as you are working this process and seeing the World in a new way!

<u>The below concepts will be very useful in any of your relationships.</u>

Concept #21

Life is a projection of your beliefs – ***Michael Cavallaro***

We project our view of the world onto other people and they become like movie screens we are watching. We can only see the world in the way we believe it exists. If we don't believe it, how can we see it and know what it is? If you believe the world is a hostile place, then you will see it as hostile. If you believe it is unfair, then you will see it as unfair.

In general, you will see the world based on your environment and the way your parents see it. There are individual beliefs, family of origin beliefs and humankind beliefs that all influence the way we see the world. We must break free of all these to be full creators.

As part of your new changes you must be open to seeing and responding to things in a new way. At times, you may find yourself using old beliefs or thoughts in your present day. When and if you do, please keep in mind this is simply an old habit and all that you have learned in this guide is the "new" you and you simply need to practice and apply your new wisdom. Be patient, for some of you it may take some getting used to.

Concepts #22

The only person you can change is yourself- **Michael Cavallaro**

Change yourself and your world will change too. You are the only one you can change. You can choose to change and grow or you can choose to stagnate and watch your life deteriorate. Many times, we wish others would be different so we could be happy.

As a result, we try to change other people, but it is our perceptions that make us unhappy, not their behaviors. When you finally realize that you are the creator of your world, you will recognize that you must change yourself first in order to change the way you perceive the world and the way the world is reflected back to you.

Happiness does not come from outside you, it comes from within. When you are by yourself and are satisfied with yourself, your world will begin to change. As a result, your beliefs, perceptions and your life will change. Your destiny is at your command. Are you ready to take hold and direct your destiny?

Remember you have all of your answers within you. When you find yourself trying to get something to fulfill you from others or validation from others, you are in an old belief system. Until we find that fulfillment within us we will never be satisfied. You and you alone are the source of your happiness and the creator of your experience.

Concepts #23

It's not what you say, it's how you say it and what you intend- **Michael Cavallaro**

It's not what you say, it's the words you choose, the tone of your voice and what you intend for the message to convey or feel like. It is the energy behind the words that speaks volumes. If we choose hurtful words, they will hurt and no understanding will take place. If we are loud or hostile in our voice, no one will listen and there will be no real communication. There will only be a threatening, scary situation for the other person. If we intend to hurt, it will come through in our tone and attitude and no one will hear what we were trying to say; they will only hear and feel our attack even if it is silent.

Consciously choose words that mean what you want to say and say them firmly, clearly, but gently, with the intent to express yourself to be understood. If you do this, you will be heard, people will listen and things will change. However, if you say nice words but your intent is to hurt or manipulate people will feel this. It will come through in your tone and attitude.

For example, which would you prefer to hear: "You hurt me and I don't like you." or "Your actions brought up something that was painful for me." The feeling people get from the energy behind or in your words will determine if people listen or understand you.

Concept #24

You cannot live what you do not believe- **Michael Cavallaro**

It's not possible for you to live a life that doesn't match your belief systems. If you do not believe something, then you cannot perceive it and it cannot exist in your life. Therefore, everything you do or experience in life is only possible because it is part of a belief system that you either have right now or have experienced.

Your life exists the way it does because you have beliefs that create and support it. Thus, in order to change your life, you must change your beliefs.

Keep in mind that most of your beliefs were formed as a small child, therefore the beliefs you created consciously or unconsciously are mostly flawed and inaccurate. Sometimes the ego has a hard time swallowing this fact, don't let it stop you! You were a child and had little or no experience in the world, you did nothing wrong!

Concept #25

You cannot judge what you do not know- **Michael Cavallaro**

You can only judge that which you have already experienced. Otherwise, you would see the wonder of its newness and it would have no meaning. Judgments come from your past experiences and, for the most part, are formed when you are young. Even though you are older, these judgments are still with you whether you think so or not.

Although your outlook may be different now, you are still judging everything through the eyes of the child who perceived the original event. It is important to understand this as it often leads to inaccurate and childish judgments.

What you judge is what you do yourself in some form. Most times you see it in yourself and then judge it in others. It may be in deed or in thought, either in the past or in the present, but you have participated in it at some time.

To see it, judge it or recognize it is to claim ownership of it. To judge something or someone is to say, "I am that which I judge."

Concept #26

Hurt is not getting what you want - **Michael Cavallaro**

The true definition of hurt is not getting what you want, when you want it, and how you want it. All negative feelings, whether anger, sadness, hurt, grief, denial or any others, are defined in the same way: not getting what you want. They all come from the perspective that the fulfillment of all your needs must come from outside you. The cause of all hurt or pain is unfulfilled expectations and the lack of acceptance of what is. The expectation can be anything: expecting to be loved or approved of, obtaining a new toy, car or even getting a new job. We are acting like spoiled two-year-olds throwing temper tantrums when we do this. This is not to say that this is uncommon or wrong, it is simply the behavior of a two-year-old. Human beings tend to want what they want, when they want it, and if they don't get it, they are hurt, sad, depressed or angry. Anytime they don't like something, they have chosen not to accept the situation as it is. As a result, most humans do not form the skill of unconditional acceptance.

When other people disappoint you, realize that it's because you expect them to be something that they are not. The next time you get angry or upset, ask what is it that you didn't get that you wanted. If you truly understand this concept, your entire outlook on life will be altered.

Concept #27

See what it is you really see, not what you want to see - **Michael Cavallaro**

Look for fact and truth in all that you see and do. This means learning to see beyond your limited perceptions, so you can see what is actually occurring; not what you think is occurring or what you have made up. Most humans see what they want to see because it fits and justifies their reality. In other words, what they see supports their belief systems, whatever they may be. These systems are then reinforced by not seeing the truth. If a person sees the truth, it may not match his or her patterned beliefs and therefore can cause internal conflict. This usually turns into denial or repression of what is true. It takes people with inner courage to look at what truly is and face themselves as well as their false realities. Not seeing the truth keeps you from looking at your issues and keeps you trapped in your patterns. Have the courage to look and sight will be granted. When sight is granted, then the choice becomes yours. Remember, it is you who grants the sight, not some mysterious force. This will begin the end of your unhappiness.

Concept #28

Birds of a Feather, flock together- **Michael Cavallaro**

Pay attention to the friends and people you surround yourself with. You can learn about your issues and what level of consciousness you are at by looking at the issues and consciousness of your friends, family and acquaintances. The energy or issues that they carry are the same or similar to yours in some respect. You are attracted to people with like energy or issues. If your energy or issues were not similar, you would be repelled by each other.

When you are judging those around you, you must remember that they are like you in some way or you would not be with them.

You surround yourself with people who are like you or have similar energies, even if they look different on the surface. So, remember that when you are judging those around you, you are actually judging yourself.

The 55 Concepts

In this guide, we share with you only 29 of the 55 Concepts that are in the book, *"The 55 Concepts – A Guide To Conscious Living"* **by Michael Cavallaro.** If you want to learn about the other concepts, the book can be downloaded from our website or purchased on Amazon.

Once you have opened your eyes to these concepts and your own patterns, you will begin seeing them everywhere; what you do, where you go, in others.

It actually is quite amusing when these concepts start to show up in your life.

You'll wonder how you never noticed them before. This is what happens when you become conscious.

<u>Being unconscious is a funny thing</u>

When one starts to become conscious, there will be times when you will want to slip into being ignorant. You will fool yourself into thinking that ignorance is blissful. This is simply not true! But it certainly feels that way.

It's so easy to fall asleep. It's really true, sometimes you will just want to fall back asleep into an unconsciousness state.

Don't!
But if you do, don't judge yourself.
It is what it is.

Be aware of what's ahead.
See it coming.
Stay conscious!

Not like Dorothy, Scarecrow, Tin Woodsmen and the Lion
in the poppy field just before reaching OZ.

YOU are just reaching OZ!

Consciousness takes Commitment.

If you decide to go or remain unconscious, at least, be honest with yourself. Admit it to yourself that you are consciously choosing to go there.

Remember NO keeping SECRETS to yourself anymore!
Don't judge where you are at any given time, just admit where you are!

If you need a break, and want to enter into unconsciousness, know that you are playing in the matrix and are subject to the results of your beliefs and patterned behaviors. In other words, you are controlled by a predictable future.

We understand that this journey can seem challenging.

But we can assure you the rewards far outweigh the challenges.

Most people believe that they cannot stay conscious because they perceive that the awakening is painful or difficult. During the awakening period, it can sometimes feel that way. There is a lot of stretching and expanding and a lot of admitting of things, which can be perceived as painful.

Keep in mind that the pain is merely the ego losing hold of you and its control of your experience. At this point the ego becomes like a spoiled child. It will attempt in every way to get you to quit, divert or distract you by telling you that you can't do it, you shouldn't do it, it will be hard or painful so why bother, you will never succeed etc.

This is very common just before things are about to change.
From experience, we can tell you that it is worth sticking it out!

Push through this stage and you will be greatly rewarded.
You will see and experience the world differently.

Tips on doing your belief work.

1. Make sure if you are using our Belief Change Package that you follow the directions exactly.

2. If using another system, investigate it and consult other users.

3. Focus completely on what you are doing.

4. <u>Remember to trail ALL beliefs to the earliest time you can remember.</u>

5. <u>Be open and at the very least – Be neutral - when doing it.</u>

Believing in the process is not necessary for it to work.

Just do it…watch it work!

The Forgotten Partner

Partnering Up

The Forgotten and Often Ignored Victim

<u>What about Partner Love?</u>

The Ones Who Love The Abused/Traumatized Person

Michael: Partners of abused or traumatized people, from now on referred to as ATP, have their own plight, which is seldom, if at all recognized. So here it is for them!

Hats off to you for being a partner and for hanging in there with all of your love, your patience and willingness to endure!

Adele: Yes, thanks to all of you!

Michael: These individuals:

- Regularly pay a high emotional price for all the abusers, experiences and misinterpretations of the past!
- Are seen as both the saviors of love and the abuser at any given moment!

- Are rarely thanked and appreciated for all they do and for being willing and loving enough to stay when everyone else is distanced, driven away or avoided!

Here we have called these people victims and you might wonder why.

Well, let me tell you....

Partners are victimized by the beliefs, programs and patterns of the abused! They are at times blamed, held accountable, resented, attacked, projected upon, dumped on and assaulted energetically and unjustly by the belief system of the ATP simply because they are present. All the while, the ATP feels justified in doing so and may at times feel bad afterward.

We want you to know this is common. But we also want you to know this is unfair and unloving! We want you to know that this assault on a truly caring individual can make them seem uncaring and anything else you want them to look like.

This assault on their being can make them frustrated, angry, disappointed, depressed, anxious, distant or shut down, which will prove to the ATP that this person is bad for them or even worse....abusive, when in fact none of this may be true at all.

Yet this type of treatment will trigger the partners own issues and beliefs about self, family patterns and being loved which will create responses from them such as: withdrawal, distancing, arguing, looking for love or happiness elsewhere.

You see, typically the ATP (Abused Traumatized Person) has decided that it is not safe to be loved, people are dangerous or they do not deserve love; therefore, unconsciously they want to keep everyone at a safe distance and if anyone gets too close, they make sure they drive them away to a safe distance again.

It is not because it is what they really want, but it is because they have a belief system that tells them this is the only safe way to exist.

Adele: This sounds pretty bleak....

Michael: It can be at times and yet it does build a beautiful strength in the relationship in order to withstand the assault.

You know, kinda like when you tell me what I should eat something that is healthy instead of the chocolate that I love. I resist your assault and I have gained great strength to resist you even more the next time…hahahaha!

Anyway… by proving they will not leave, the ATP may often create a great trust in the relationship.

Adele: True! And real funny, Michael!

Michael: You must understand that because you are an ATP, there is a high likelihood your perceptions are off/inaccurate, especially when you are emotional.

Adele: Maybe it would be helpful to know why we choose certain partners - Intimate, business or friends. Choosing a certain partner is very purposeful on an unconscious level for everyone, but especially so for the ATP.

Michael: Yes, that is correct. You choose them unconsciously for many reasons but there are three key ones:

1. Because they will allow you to run from your belief, and patterns.
2. Because they will make you face your beliefs and patterns.
3. Because they will support your beliefs and patterns.

Adele: Patience please!

Michael: That reminds me - Partners need clear accurate communication in order to understand what is happening to the ATP.

Adele: Yes, Michael needed a lot of that. As long as I communicated with him, he was fine but when I didn't communicate or shut him out, things got fugly.

Michael: So because of my personal experience and being a counselor, I felt that this chapter was a must for everyone!

Your Partner

Anyway, here's some information specifically for the partners standing next to someone who had been abused. But those of you working the guide, we want you to really get this information too and remember your partner has many challenges as they stand beside you and love you the best they can!

Don't make your home your emotional litter box - Concept #13 – this was mentioned earlier in the book. This one is huge, but almost all people ignore it at some point in their lives. A litter box is where a cat leaves its excrement. You often leave your emotional excrement at home and are nicer to strangers or people you do not live with. You carry around your stresses all day and then you go home and release them.

For example, you may be short-tempered, impatient, grumpy or intolerant when you get home at the end of a day and then wonder why home is so unpleasant. If you come home and yell at your children, ignore your spouse or demand things in a rude way, is it any wonder that the feelings at home are combative, hostile or empty? Is it any wonder people at home would be less than welcoming? As a result, work, friends, school or anywhere else becomes the place you would rather be. Home becomes the dreaded place; other places become your haven.

Home should be your haven. Home should be a place where everyone feels safe. You are often kinder and more patient with strangers, acquaintances, co-workers and friends than with your children or spouse. Shouldn't your partner or children be treated with special care? Always treat those you love with kindness and respect.

Pattern Compatibility

Do your patterns play well with others?

In life, you have to get along with people and their patterns in order to enjoy their essence and the human experience.

If you do not get along with them, you cannot enjoy them because your patterns conflict; you cannot be together and/or you won't like each other.

Example: If there are two people and one is a demanding personality and the other a sensitive personality, they would get irritated with each other at some point and they won't get along. The sensitive person is constantly annoyed and hurt by the demanding person and doesn't want to talk to them while the demanding person gets tired of dealing with the sensitive person's feelings.

How could you ever see the beauty in the other person, if there was this constant struggle between you?

So, you see, it is not just that the people must like each other but that their patterns must be able to play together nicely in order to have a relationship.

Michael: Most people in relationships cannot see what is happening clearly due to their issues. especially when they misperceive what is really happening and make up stories about what they are seeing and feeling, without even checking with their partner. All too often people hear the words of another and then make up their own understanding about what that person means. We can guarantee you that if you do this, you will be inaccurate 75% of the time.

It would behoove you to learn to ask questions rather than assume understandings. When you assume understanding, you are using your own conscious and unconscious interpretations to understand what another person is thinking or feeling. The truth is what they are feeling is not your experience.

So, the best advice that we can give you is to ask the other person exactly what they mean when they say something. By asking this question you are not only honoring the other person, but you are also seeking truth and accuracy versus relying on your own outdated belief system to tell you what someone else is feeling or experiencing. 90% of any fights or arguments will be due to misunderstandings and misinterpretations of what the other person is saying or intending to communicate. It is imperative that you begin to ask your partner or anyone, for that matter, to define for you what they actually mean whenever you are in any emotional or heated conversation.

In general conversation, where there is not this intensity, it is still wise for you to ask them to define what they mean even if you are sure of what they are saying. This will seem awkward in the beginning, but it will assure that you will have a common understanding and language with the person you are communicating with. Eventually you will not need to ask them to clarify because from your history you will have had these discussions previously and have accomplished a baseline understanding without assumption.

Most people think listening is hearing other people's words and making up your own meaning of what they said. This is actually the most likely way to create misunderstandings and difficulties.

- Never assume you know what someone is saying.

- Always ask for clarity until you have that baseline communication that we spoke of a moment ago.

- Always ask for clarity when you are in an emotional state or heatedly intense conversation. This is because these are the most common times people make misinterpretations based upon their own patterns and belief system thereby creating problems that do not exist. You can save yourself and your partner much grief and aggravation by doing so.

How do our patterns influence our partnerships?

Let's take a common way people look for a partner. This technique is where you write down a list of the desired qualities of your partner. I want them handsome, beautiful, smart, tall, short, kind, friendly, common interests etc.

Where do you think all these qualities come from?

Your belief systems of course!

Here you are, in this technique choosing the qualities of a partner from your belief systems. What do you think that the likelihood of this partner having issues that relate to you or your patterns is?
Why 100%, of course!

In this case, you are choosing a partner based on your patterns, behaviors and belief systems. When you have issues with your partner, you might wonder where they come from or why are things so difficult.

Well the answer is very simple: You chose them and they match your patterns and belief systems, thereby reflecting to you all of the issues about yourself that you are either aware of or unconscious of. This can make for quite an active relationship. So in the good times, these matching patterns are wonderful. But in the bad times, they are stressful.

Remember: you chose them!

And then there are these types of beliefs that lead to relationships: I only get involved with adversarial relationships, abusive relationships, non-communicative relationships, partners who don't understand me, partners who don't stick up for themselves, partners who are bossy, partners who are strong-willed, partners who are passive etc.

This batch is based upon previous experiences that have become belief systems and truths that dictate your conscious and unconscious choosing of a partner. Now, it is also possible that you have chosen a partner who is actually a perfect match but because of your belief system, you cannot see who they truly are; therefore, you create difficulties and challenges that actually do not exist.

The major point to all this is that you pick your partner for multiple reasons and unless you take the time to see through your own delusional realities to find out who your partner is, all of your judgments about your partner are potentially made up, not real, or distorted at best.

Take the time to get to know your partner intimately and from what is going on inside of them, not from what is going on inside of you. We sometimes refer to them as the forgotten partner because the ATP sees their partner through their own distortions and does not know truly who their partner is or know the heart of their partner.

It takes extra work to get to know the heart of your partner and intimately understand them versus understand them from your perspective. Do not forget them, remember to discover who they are and this will ensure a much healthier relationship and possibly even take a great burden off of yourself.

Love me for who I am

Adele: Remember this statement earlier? I said I would talk about it in a later chapter. Well it's time!!

For me, I searched for someone who would love me unconditionally. I wanted someone who would love me, just for me. What does that even mean? I wanted someone who would love the love that I have inside, and not just for my body or what I could do for them.

Now, just making that statement makes me laugh.

Can you see how confusing that could get for a partner who loves you <u>AND</u> your body?
And what's wrong with them loving you and your body? Somehow when you're wounded you believe that they shouldn't love your body, it is somehow derogatory. This is often because the ATP hates or despises their own body and can find no love for it and unconsciously or consciously they do not want anyone to love it or them.

Then there is the whole concept of having sex with your partner and considering it to be work or a chore. What a very strange concept for people who love each other.

Imagine thinking this:

"I love my partner but I find it repulsive to touch their skin and be physically close to them."

Many wounded people actually think this.

Here's another one: "The thought of having physical pleasure and feeling love with my partner is disgusting and takes too much effort.

That sounds ridiculous if you think about it. But I have heard many women say this.

Concept #29

There are no relationship Issues, only individual ones- **Michael Cavallaro**

Issues belong to individuals, not to couples or relationships. If an individual does not have an issue, then the couple does not have one. Relationships of all kinds merely give you the opportunity to see your own issues. Relationships are <u>learning vehicles</u>. You choose your partners consciously and unconsciously because they match your beliefs and understanding of the world. This means that their behaviors, the ones you see and the ones you don't, are in line with your beliefs somehow.

As a simplified example, if you believe that men are mean, then you will attract a mean man. He may be mean verbally or mean by withdrawing, but either way, he will have mean intents or actions. If you believe that relationships do not last, then you will attract people who will not be compatible and believe the same, or drive away those who are compatible. You do not make it happen intentionally, but rather unconsciously. This is also called a self-fulfilling prophecy or self-sabotage. In fact, there is no such thing as self-sabotage; there is only the fulfillment of a pattern.

You may find it easier to be alone because there is no one to reflect your issues back to you. If you had acne and no mirror, would you notice your acne as much? Of course not. In the same way, others mirror your issues back to you, but you often forget this and blame them for your pain.

A peak healthy relationship in human form looks like two individuals working on their own issues, confiding and working together to assist each other in both managing the issues and resolving them as they go through them while enjoying the relationship. This is not to say that in a relationship the partner will not do things that irritate you or push your buttons. It is to remember that when they push your buttons remember that they are your buttons and if you did not have the button to begin with, there would be nothing to push. So no matter how much your partner pushes, unless you have the buttons there is no effect

So, when this does occur, remember back to concept number one: anything that bothers you is your issue. Remember, all your feelings are all about you. You are the center of your universe, the source from which all of your feelings and perceptions emanate.

Adele: I had to keep reminding myself of this concept. When I had an issue with Michael, it had always related to me. Not to say, that Michael was perfect by no means! (Ha!) I have to say, Michael, if you could improve anything on your end, you always would. You always checked yourself first.

Michael: Why thank you. It is always all about us, both the positive and negatively perceived experience.

Remember all human beings do things for themselves, not to other people.

Adele: Yes, *people don't do things to you, they do them for themselves.* They didn't do it TO me. They did it for THEMSELVES! this is helpful in an intimate partnership. This was one concept that really changed things for me.

As you have read, I did a lot of projecting my beliefs onto others and also was very tuned into how the world (the things outside of me) would respond to me.

I simply made up beliefs about what males were supposed to feel like – creepy, only wanting sex, selfish and liars.

I believed that men were wimps (sorry guys) and <u>if I wanted something done, I had to do it myself</u>.

Another belief that I had about males was that joking meant you were making fun of me or disregarding me. My dad had a great sense of humor, (I was told) but I couldn't see the humor. I only saw the cutting edge. I became a very serious person, especially with males, as a way to protect my heart, avoid feeling, and deguise my anger from all of my past wounds.

Michael: Adele, you do know that seriousness is only the positive aspect of anger which allows you to look like a nice person even though you are pissed off at the world.

Adele: Yeah yeah, whatever, Michael. LOL! He had worked on me for years, to give up my anger and stubborn ways. I can't tell you how many times he would just laugh at myself! I was very skilled at ignoring his constant joking.

The Courage - Michael and I

At first, I didn't know what to expect from being with a man:

- Who was very aware
- Was always working on himself
- Was very clear in what he wanted
- Communicated well

…AND had a kind heart.

I learned quickly, yet I struggled a lot adjusting to this relationship. I knew that sex would be required. But that was an easy fix; I knew how to leave my body during those times and just pretend I was there. Did I have orgasms, yes, but it started in my head - I would constantly go in and out.

Michael, being the feeler that he was, would take notice and of course, express when he felt me leaving my body. I couldn't pretend because he was too observant. I couldn't hide the fact that I was leaving my body. Today it's almost funny to think about.

He would say, "Where ya going?"
Ugh…how embarrassing!

Although, Thank God for him, right? Now I can be present during an intimate encounter.

Michael: An intimate encounter?

Adele: Sex, making love, an intimate experience – you know what I mean, ya weirdo! See what I have to put up with!

Michael and Adele: A LOL together moment.

Adele: I share with you these private details to show you how my beliefs were running the show. I wanted you to understand and feel the old Adele and now see the new me!

Even though Michael was the safest that I had ever felt with anyone, I actually still couldn't stay present with him all the time – in and outside of the bedroom, no matter how kind he was.

So, revealing my secrets was a reoccurring thing that happened frequently in our relationship. He was almost always present. Again, I couldn't hide or control anything. So, my controlled experience method, just wasn't happening.

He taught me a lot in the first five years of our marriage. It was tough, but he was very kind.

Michael: Well, let's be honest, Adele. What would you frequently say to me? "You are required to be patient with me, Michael!"

Adele: Oh, yeah, that's right!

Michael: I learned an equal number of things from Adele. Like for instance, how not to close my heart, patience, fortitude, gentleness and so much more. It took a lot of getting used to.

We had to accept and appreciate our approaches on a number of things:

- Communication
- Behaviors
- Emotions
- Beliefs.

Thank god that's over!

Communication is Key

When others perceive, what you say and do through an issue that is theirs, it typically elicits hurt of some kind.

The truth does not hurt, only people's refusal to see it and their unwillingness to look within hurts. Wanting to remain in a falsehood is what causes the pain. Truth is truth; there is no emotion in truth, although if you judge truth it may cause pain. This judgment creates many complications.

Of course, it is your responsibility as a partner/friend to deliver your truth kindly. Sometimes, calling each other out may not sound kind, but as partners/friends you have to have an understanding and love for each other, that you are willing to unconditionally accept the other partner's human's thoughts, feelings, emotions, behaviors, family patterning, belief system and perceived faults. You are not your behaviors and you are NOT all these things that I mentioned above.

12 Keys to Transformation While in an Intimate Relationship

1. Honesty – both with self and partner
2. Clear Communication
3. Never Blame
4. Own Your Feelings
5. Awareness – of yourself, your triggers, your behaviors, your choices and your intent.
6. Be Open to Feedback from Your Partner
7. Self-Reflection
8. Expressing Your Fears and the Purpose behind Your Behaviors or Words.
9. Own Your Mistakes and Misinterpretations.
10. Express Your Gratitude for Your Partner's Patience and Assistance.
11. Express Your Desire of How You Would like the Relationship to Look and Feel.
12. Express and Act With a Willingness to Change.

Chapter Eight
SUMMARY

- **Seven Steps to Freedom (7)** - Clearing Your Beliefs

- Belief Package

- Re-entering the Matrix

- The Forgotten Partner

- **Concept #20:** *Life is a Projection of Your Beliefs*

- **Concept # 21:** *The only person you can change is yourself. Life is a projection of your beliefs.*

- **Concept #22:** *It's not what you say, it's how you say it and what you intend.*

- **Concept # 23:** *You cannot live what you do not believe*

- **Concept #24:** *You cannot judge what you do not know*

- **Concept # 25:** *You cannot live what you do not believe*

- **Concept #26:** *Hurt is Not Getting What you Want*

- **Concept #27:** *See what it is you really see, not what you want to see*

- **Concept # 28:** *Birds of a Feather Flock Together*

- **Concept #29:** *There are no relationship issues only individual ones*

- **Exercise Y:** List some of the beliefs that you have discovered about yourself.

Chapter Nine

Our Final Thoughts

Exercise Z

If you could create/experience whatever you wanted
(without limitations) what would that be?

Searching For Oz Guidebook

Remember the concept in chapter six, *We only chase what we believe that we do not have,* and then we asked you to list the things that you desire and/or still chase? It is now time to do belief work on this topic. It's time to rid yourself of these desires.

Why? You might ask!

Why would I want to get rid of those desires? Great question! You want to get rid of them because they came from a mentality of "I don't have them," simply because you think of these things, it indicates your belief in not having them. It is making the statement, "I want the things I do not have," instead of coming from the mindset that I will remember that I already have them or I will get to re-experience them.

Desire indicates that belief in lack or not having of whatever it is you desire. How can you get/acquire that which you believe you don't have.

OUR FINAL THOUGHTS

You have just learned our **Six Stages of our Abuse & Recovery System, Seven Steps to Freedom, 29 Concepts and worked through Exercises from A to Z!.**

How do you feel? Are you healed yet?!

Well, parts of you are!

Discoveries were made, secrets were revealed and processes were laid out. Now how about going ALL the Way! Remember the different types of people that we had described earlier regarding how one unravels their own ball of yarn?

Which will you be?

Now that you know there is nothing to be afraid of, we suggest that you start unraveling!

Adele's final thoughts

I now see life through a different lens.

I have passion for this growth that I have achieved. I no longer feel the need to minimize my passion and love for anything or anyone. I have no need to protect myself. I am enough.

- My mind is clear about the traumas and has clarity beyond most, about this subject.
- I feel safe internally and externally.
- My mind no longer plays tricks on me regarding my fear of the betrayal of another, as well as, being abused again.
- I no longer have fear that another has the power to take advantage of me.
- I cannot be duped, surprised or be taken advantage of.

Here's how I am different:

Your Past

So, you looked at your past, well, more like - you glanced at your past. This is only the beginning of YOU getting to know YOU.

We have shown you the foundation of how you were put together - Your very own building blocks of your beliefs and Identities.

Think of it this way: You now have the keys to physically walk out of the witch's castle of fear, shame or guilt etc.- to freedom beyond your limitations.

Do these exercises like your life depended on it for each fear, hurt, shame, guilt that comes your way!

Don't stop until you get this freedom...because you deserve it!

You are making your way home (to yourself) to being truly free!

Remember Keep No Secrets

Nothing is a secret!

I mean nothing!

When everything's out in the open and no surprises or embarrassments affect you any longer, you begin to feel more comfortable with you and your world.

Imagine a life that is not controlled - a life that you can live in the present peacefully.

You may not obtain this peace right away.
You will need to apply the tools in your life to get there.
If you apply the tools in your every waking hour, you get there quicker. It's as simple as that! If you apply the tools some of the time, not so much.

I have been observing this process for years, and what I am saying to you is fact because I have witnessed it. I have watched people transform and find their inner voice.

Those that apply will get there.
-
It just depends on how bad you want it.

How bad do you want it?!

In the beginning, when Michael first introduced this process to me, I didn't believe that I feel the way I do today! I just wanted to feel better and make this second marriage work.

In the beginning, I saw the love of the big picture. I saw and loved Michael's bigness and admired the amount of work that he had done and was still doing on himself. It felt good to be next to him and he treated me with such love.

But did I think that I could get to where he was and see how big I was? Absolutely not - no matter how many times Michael would tell me that I could.

So, with that said, I only applied the tools, some of the time, just enough to get by. Each time, I carved and chiseled out some of my belief system and patterning that lay stuck inside, and each time I saw another opening, experiencing a peace that I never felt before.

There was a point that I got over the hump, like I said before in the earlier chapters of this guide. After that, it started to get easier. Everyone does it differently regarding the way in which they use the tools. Some are fast and some just do enough to get by. But either way you choose.

There comes a time when you reach the point where it shifts and it gets easier.

It's like at the beginning of the pre-season for those of you who are athletes out there. The first two weeks, getting into shape, is hell!

Well, I will say to you, give it two years. Now you may say, TWO years?! What, Adele?!

Yes, two years to get over the hump where life becomes smoother and happier.

Come on! I am asking you to give yourself two years out of HOW many years you have left here on earth, 30, 40, 50?

<u>Aren't you worth it?</u>

I plan to teach the children of the next generation that they do not have to please anyone, only themselves and also, that love comes from within. No searching necessary. I searched for a very long time, only to find that <u>I had it within me all the time!</u>

Imagine, teaching the next generation this process in their first six years of life?! Well you can!

Michael once wrote this: There are 3 things a child needs before the age of 5.

1. Knowing they are loved
2. Knowing they are heard
3. Knowing they have the right to speak and express themselves

This is the knowing in their heart, not in their mind. They know not because they were told these things but because they truly know themselves from their core.

It is the job of a parent to make sure their child has these 3 foundational knowings!

Do you have these knowings or are they only mental?

Does your child have these knowings or are they only mental?

You can talk and write on this subject about the parent-child connection all you want and it sounds really good in theory, but can a parent really deliver to the child the following:

1. Give pure unconditional LOVE.
2. Truly listen to the heart of a child and what they are saying.
3. Teach the child that they have a right to speak during their foundational base years.

Is a parent able to deliver this while having beliefs and identities of their own? I don't know. But what I do know is this:

Michael experimented with this process when his children (my step-children) were young. It wasn't perfect, to say the least, because the process wasn't very developed yet. But what I do notice is the difference in these children when it comes to unconditional love from dad, knowing that they are heard and that they have a right to speak. This does not mean they always agree.

I have tested this group of family members again and again, and what always seems to remain consistent is the fact that they know that they are Love by one anothert. They know they are heard and that they have the right to speak.

This does not mean that they all believe that others will accept and give love unconditionally, will hear them or when they speak (because they know that they have a right to speak) or that they will be listened to by others. They just know that among the five of them (The four children and Dad) that these three things are present and will always stay true because it was modelled and taught since birth. Again, birth to six years old is the crucial time for the creation of beliefs and Identities.

Read, *"Change Your Mind, Not your Child,"* **by Michael Cavallaro** for additional information about raising conscious children.

The Glow

There is a peace, more like a glow, that hovers over you, when you make it over that hump. It's an awesome feeling.

You have all the tools that were given to you and you just have to apply them when needed. But you need all the tools!

If you find yourself wanting to skip a step, just know, this process will not be as effective.

Admittance of certain parts of your life occurs all throughout this process. You just have to be ready for it when it shows up. Again, if you have the tools and the basics, it is so much easier.

If you don't apply all the tools, you will tend to fight and struggle.

Being Honest

Being honest with yourself will be the most difficult part for you.

Every piece of the trauma and how you felt about it and what beliefs you chose to keep should be looked at. <u>I am talking about the subtleties now.</u>

You should almost be relentless when searching for those hidden pieces. Most people from the outside, meaning people that are not on this journey, will believe that these parts are unnecessary. This is the stage that you have to decide whether you want to just live with the guilt, shame, fear that you have remaining or completely be free from all your limitations.

For me, there was no in between. You either had the guilt or you didn't. I didn't want it any more.

<u>I wanted to be free from it!</u>

What I am talking about here is the beginning of a journey of true internal transformation/healing. To be honest with you, if I didn't see the miracles of this freedom, I wouldn't have believed it and I wouldn't have participated for as long as I have.

You see, once you know how to dismantle these perceived beliefs, it's quite easy and freeing to reveal things about yourself. I had to be aware of every thought, feeling and behavior during this process.

Was I self-abusing. Yes!

Michael: You must know the difference between mourning and wallowing in the identity of victim. Start using victim as an adjective not a noun. Based upon an event it is not a noun and should NEVER become your identity.

You should never use the phrase victim if you want to heal, but instead say, I perceived I was victimized in that event in that experience.

I want you to consider something. If you lock yourself into any identity, then you most likely will not have the freedom that you are searching for. That IS why you picked up this book, right?

Adele: Wait, Michael, I am in the middle of my Inner-Thoughts section of chapter nine.

Michael: Wait…do I have an Inner Thoughts Section?

Adele: Oh, I am not sure yet. I didn't finish the guide yet. I'll let you know soon! :) Just kidding. Of course you get a section, Darling!

Michael: Well okay, then. Let me just say one thing here.

You could clear up many things in your head, such as your emotions but still, physically, sense and feel the memories that lay dormant right underneath your skin. Literally, right under your skin!

Memories of touch, smell and sound are just as bothersome. These things are literally, in your cell memory. No worries. This takes time and application to dismantle the judgment of these memories.

Facing Myself and My Experiences

Adele: I am back. I just threw Michael out of my Inner Thoughts section. :)

Taking the time and being committed to facing myself was imperative in this process. All the years that I have been applying this process, I tried very hard not to say that something was completely finished.

There is always more to learn. But after you get over that hump, it will make everything so much easier. Mastering some of these tools, brings you to a new level of living. Just know, there is always more. I seriously had to truly want these patterns to be gone from the bottom of my soul (whatever that means). It just sounded really good when I typed it.

I couldn't even want these feelings a little. Remember, these feelings and charges of emotions come from a belief system, family patterning (and soul memory) that were introduced to me at a very young age.

There is a process that you need to go through in order to release them.

With that being said, there's not a manual to dismantle these beliefs because each one of us is unique. Each of us has created a certain set of beliefs in a unique way, forming a web.

Each one of you has to learn your own web and how it was designed; how you put it together. You then begin to untie the knots and entangle what you created and trail back to find those beliefs that you created at a very young age.

Bam! There you have it! Undo those beliefs and start living free!
It's simple and yet it's not. I look at it now as simple. But in the beginning and sometimes, in the middle, I found it very difficult. It wasn't until the pain of the abuse in my head stood out more than the pain of the process.

<u>When the desire to change outweighs the pain, is when you will stick with this process!</u>

This process was worth every second of my time!

I find it fascinating at the pace at which a person enters this process to untangle their own web. Some do it rapidly. Some, not so much. Some only pick out certain ones to release.

Up until I wrote this guide, I pretty much looked on everything and everyone in my life, except for some threads of feelings and beliefs that I had about the abusers in my life. I healed some big stuff while I was writing the *Searching for OZ* book.

Writing *Searching for OZ* was an expression of me, a celebration of completing me to be free from the pain that I had endured as a human (*this lifetime*)

Funny, one of my favorite albums that I would listen to as a little girl, was called *Free to Be You and Me, by Marlo Thomas.* You know that lady, she does the St. Jude's advertisement. I actually met her father at a show that my parents took us to up in the poconos! I don't know why I just told you that. Actually, I wanted this guide to be a conversation between you and me. I wanted to share with you my every thought about my freedom and maybe just maybe, you will know that it's possible. So, as Marlo's album says, Let's be "Free To Be…You and Me!"

<u>I have gained wisdom about the deepest love, respect, honor and acceptance of myself.</u>

<u>This was my experience and I honor myself and the effort of this life's journey.</u>

Okay Michael, your section begins now!

Michael's Inner Thoughts

Michael: Well my apologies, Adele, for invading your inner thoughts section. I didn't realize I was going to have my own inner thoughts section in the book.
Adele: Well maybe it's my turn to invade your inner thoughts.

Michael: okay go for it…

Adele: Nevermind, I was just messing with you.

Michael: I did however enjoy your inner thoughts, Adele. I think they will be very interesting for people who read this book.

My inner thoughts probably won't be as exciting compared to Adele' storytellings. But what I would like to say is that all the work in the guide was quite a pleasure to create. To discover and understand how human beings work to their core and be able to share with everyone that they can change their own lives is awesome.

Keep in mind that your life's journey is always all about you. This does however mean, you should be kind in all things, be respectful of others but most of all, be respectful of yourself.

When you give up the respect and honoring of yourself, you are subject to the belief systems of others. This is known as giving your power away. I would like to say that there is no such thing as giving your power away. So, if anyone says you are giving your power away, please run from them because they do not understand what actually is at work here.

It is impossible for you to give your power away.

It is only possible to create an illusion that you no longer have any creative power in your life. The power others speak of is more about forcefulness and control. The power we speak of is your creative power, the ability to create.

Love yourself above all else and everything else will feel your love.

This is the greatest gift you can give to the world.

It is not your job to take care of the world nor to heal it. It is however your journey to become the love and creator of your own experience.

Keep in mind that no one is better, only different.

I didn't understand this fully until later in life. But when I finally truly got this my life completely changed.

In writing this guide and creating this work, I hope that you find your own inner peace, fulfillment and self-love, so you can live out your life here on earth as joyfully as possible and that when it is time for you to leave, you know you have been fulfilled.

This work was designed to be as simple and quick as possible.

The processes of transformation in this guide are to be used as exactly as we have shared them. This is not to be rigid, it is however to tell you that this way works. Additional modifications will create variables that may or may not produce the same results. Feel free however to experiment as you wish but know that your results may not be the same.

Everyone is ready in their own time and everyone has their own unique journey, so even in using this process of transformation, it does not guarantee the exact same results for every individual.

We have used this process with hundreds and hundreds of people successfully. All had similar outcomes but varied based upon their own souls journey and personal programming. The key to the success is application. This is not intellectual information to be read and put away. This is information to be used, applied and experienced. It is only through the experience that your own wisdom and change will come.

I myself have used all of these tools. There have been many variations and changes during the evolution of this transformational process. All of which have led to the guide you are reading.

My experience is over 40 years of application personally and over 30 years of working with others. We have done the best that we can to explain this process in words in a guide form.

This process is difficult enough to explain when you can share feeling along with the words it can be fully understood and appreciated. Our intent is to present to the world this information so that it may be used and experienced to bring about whatever the individual using it desires, in the way of self-love and improvement of life experience.

**We wish for you everything that you wish for yourself.
May each one of you find your own fulfillment
and pleasure in your life experience.**

Most of all may you find the love that you truly are.

Love Michael & Adele

PEACE

If you have any questions, please contact us
through our website www.adeleandmichael.com.

If you find you need assistance, please use our services,
if you feel that it is right for you.
adele@adeleandmichael.com

Adele Saccarelli-Cavallaro

After struggling with Dyslexia, auditory processing, ADHD and sexual abuse, Adele searched for and then co-created with her partner, Michael, processes that could help her to live a life unhindered by trauma.

In 2000, she founded the non-profit, Teamwork Wins, a Foundation of Awareness and Change, which focuses on assisting those with Invisible Challenges™ to become self-directed, free-thinking and creative individuals.

Adele is an author, speaker, artist and coach, drawing on her life experiences in teaching in the public school, coaching collegiate volleyball, presenting at schools, sports teams, businesses and prisons, life coaching/consulting, as well as directing educational programs about Invisible Challenges™ how to cope with and change them.

Currently, Adele's focus has been on her recently published work, Searching for Oz: a flowing tale of a woman finding herself again in the form of a modern day fairytale. The story embodies the same magic of the original. Dottie quiets her thinking mind, moves forward with courage & reconnects with her heart to integrate childhood trauma. It is a fictional story written through the lens of the Wonderful Wizard of Oz. The novel follows Dottie on a personal journey of finding the love of her life and the self-love that precedes it.

She also facilitates video-online coursework with this revolutionary guide Searching for OZ – The Journey Home, to assist others in finding their own answers.

Adele is a mother of two, stepmom to four and Nonna to four grandchildren. She loves to pastel as well as, travel with her husband, Michael, as well as explore the beauty and stillness of life.

www.adeleandmichael.com
www.teamworkwins.org

Michael Cavallaro

Michael Cavallaro is an author, artist, mentor, coach and speaker who has dedicated his life to finding simple, practical tools for making permanent change. He has 40+ years of experience coaching, and has helped thousands of clients to look deeper within themselves and find answers that work for them.

As an international speaker, Michael has lectured worldwide in such places as England, New Zealand, and in the US. He facilitates teamwork seminars, couples/marriage workshops, mediation and coaching, personal development classes, as well as individual sessions. He has worked with CEO's, VP's, HR, managers, entrepreneurs, coaches, therapists, teachers, trainers, sales professionals, parents, executives, lawyers, judges, couples and more.

Michael is the author of several books that help people in all areas of life. His first published book, "The 55 Concepts, A Guide to Conscious Living," forms the foundation for all that followed. Its concepts, while simple, have layers of meaning that take a lifetime to digest. The book has been read and practiced by people worldwide. Other books, include "Change your Mind, Not your Child", as well as the novel, "Searching for OZ."

In 2002, Michael founded "Living Concepts" (LC), a company based on Human Cosmology™ – the study of the inner dynamics and consciousness of the human being." LC provides personal, written, audio instruction on human patterning, belief systems and expanded consciousness. He currently shares a library of free material on his website and produces free live videos quarterly as a contribution to humanity. Different than a psychic or someone who channels, Michael has the self-described "clairsentient" ability to "sense and interpret the vibrational frequencies of self and others". He feels and understands the vibrational patterning of quantum physics in regards to the human being.

Michael is a father of four, stepdad to two and Pop Pop to four grandchildren. If he is not creating mix media art, you will find him traveling with his wife, Adele, and exploring unseen worlds.

www.adeleandmichael.com
www.michaelcavallaro.com

Made in the USA
Columbia, SC
23 May 2020